D1345536

Inside the Competitor's Mindset

Management on the Cutting Edge series

Abbie Lundberg, series editor

Published in cooperation with *MIT Sloan Management Review*

The AI Advantage: How to Put the Artificial Intelligence Revolution to Work
Thomas H. Davenport

The Technology Fallacy: How People Are the Real Key to Digital Transformation
Gerald C. Kane, Anh Nguyen Phillips, Jonathan Copulsky, and Garth Andrus

Designed for Digital: How to Architect Your Business for Sustained Success
Jeanne W. Ross, Cynthia Beath, and Martin Mocker

See Sooner, Act Faster: How Vigilant Leaders Thrive in an Era of Digital Turbulence
George S. Day and Paul J. H. Schoemaker

Leading in the Digital World: How to Foster Creativity, Collaboration, and Inclusivity
Amit S. Mukherjee

The Ends Game: How Smart Companies Stop Selling Products and Start Delivering Value
Marco Bertini and Oded Koenigsberg

Open Strategy: Mastering Disruption from Outside the C-Suite
Christian Stadler, Julia Hautz, Kurt Matzler, and Stephan Friedrich von den Eichen

The Transformation Myth: Leading Your Organization through Uncertain Times
Gerald Kane, Rich Nanda, Anh Nguyen Phillips, and Jonathan Copulsky

Winning the Right Game: How to Disrupt, Defend, and Deliver in a Changing World
Ron Adner

The Digital Multinational: Navigating the New Normal in Global Business
Satish Nambisan and Yadong Luo

Work without Jobs: How to Reboot Your Organization's Work Operating System
Ravin Jesuthasan and John W. Boudreau

The Future of Competitive Strategy: Unleashing the Power of Data and Digital Ecosystems
Mohan Subramaniam

Productive Tensions: How Every Leader Can Tackle Innovation's Toughest Trade-Offs
Chris B. Bingham and Rory M. McDonald

Working with AI: Real Stories of Human-Machine Collaboration
Thomas H. Davenport and Steven M. Miller

Enterprise Strategy for Blockchain: Lessons in Disruption from Fintech, Supply Chains, and Consumer Industries
Ravi Sarathy

Redesigning Work: How to Transform Your Organization and Make Hybrid Work for Everyone
Lynda Gratton

Inside the Competitor's Mindset: How to Predict Their Next Move and Position Yourself for Success
John Horn

Inside the Competitor's Mindset

How to Predict Their Next Move and Position
Yourself for Success

Professor Binmore,

Thank you for introducing me
to game theory at Michigan and

John Horn

instilling a lifelong love of the
subject !

John Horn

The MIT Press
Cambridge, Massachusetts
London, England

© 2023 John Horn

All rights reserved. No part of this book may be reproduced in any form by any electronic or mechanical means (including photocopying, recording, or information storage and retrieval) without permission in writing from the publisher.

The MIT Press would like to thank the anonymous peer reviewers who provided comments on drafts of this book. The generous work of academic experts is essential for establishing the authority and quality of our publications. We acknowledge with gratitude the contributions of these otherwise uncredited readers.

This book was set in ITC Stone Serif Std and ITC Stone Sans Std by New Best-set Typesetters Ltd. Printed and bound in the United States of America.

Library of Congress Cataloging-in-Publication Data

Names: Horn, John, author.
Title: Inside the competitor's mindset : how to predict their next move and
    position yourself for success / John Horn.
Description: Cambridge, Massachusetts : The MIT Press, [2023] | Series:
    Management on the cutting edge | Includes bibliographical references and index.
Identifiers: LCCN 2022023891 (print) | LCCN 2022023892 (ebook) |
    ISBN 9780262047883 (hardcover) | ISBN 9780262373630 (epub) |
    ISBN 9780262373647 (pdf)
Subjects: LCSH: Competition. | Industrial management. | Leadership. |
    Organizational change.
Classification: LCC HD41 .H667 2023 (print) | LCC HD41 (ebook) |
    DDC 338.5/22—dc23/eng/20220822
LC record available at https://lccn.loc.gov/2022023891
LC ebook record available at https://lccn.loc.gov/2022023892

10 9 8 7 6 5 4 3 2 1

For Maggie, Charles, Paul, and Wesley

Contents

Series Foreword

The world does not lack for management ideas. Thousands of researchers, practitioners, and other experts produce tens of thousands of articles, books, papers, posts, and podcasts each year. But only a scant few promise to truly move the needle on practice, and fewer still dare to reach into the future of what management will become. It is this rare breed of idea—meaningful to practice, grounded in evidence, and *built for the future*—that we seek to present in this series.

Abbie Lundberg

Editor in Chief
MIT Sloan Management Review

Preface

When I began helping companies design, build, and run war games—simulations to determine the best strategic course of action to take vis-à-vis their competitors—I was quickly surprised by the clients' frequent response. Many claimed we could not use war gaming exercises or that we couldn't role-play certain competitors in the workshop because those competitors were irrational. At first, I thought it was a throwaway line or a reference to the burgeoning field of behavioral economics, which highlights the foibles affecting human beings' ability to make the "correct" decision.

But as more clients kept using this particular word—irrational—I realized they were not referencing behavioral economists' theories nor were they trivially dismissing their competitors. They truly believed the competition were irrational; they could not wrap their minds around why competitors behaved the way they did. Often, the statement would be followed by "Don't they understand that's not good for the industry?" or "We would never do that."

What was curious to me was that the companies I helped were large, sophisticated players. How was it that the companies that rose to be significant competitors to those I was helping were able to do so while acting irrationally? I even heard partners at my old firm refer to their clients' competitors as irrational—even though there probably were other partners in our firm serving those exact competitors and likely sitting around with their teams calling the first client "irrational"!

What was more curious to me was that I only needed to ask a few simple questions, such as "are those choices helping them to grow?" or "how does that decision compare with what you've done in the past?" for them to explain why the moves made sense. Answers would be as simple as "yes, they're growing by stealing share from us." The client's past moves were always justified, sometimes because it would generate a competitive advantage: "it was good for us when we did it but no one else should."

This common assertion of competitor irrationality didn't align with what I heard about companies' competitive intelligence practices. Most companies assert that they regularly conduct competitive intelligence, but we often observe that those same companies are surprised by the actions and reactions of their competitors. When business leaders are surprised, what I have observed is that they tend to default to assuming the competitor made an irrational move. But this is a mental trap: it is not often the case that competitors are acting irrationally (i.e., acting against their own best interests by making choices that don't maximize their objectives or acting in a completely random manner). It's that we have a hard time viewing the market environment from their perspective, therefore making it hard to understand why they act the way they do.

By applying some relatively simple techniques, companies can gain much better insight into what their competitors are likely to do and thereby be better prepared when it is time to act (and react) in the competitive market. You probably have come across similar techniques in other venues, and even used some yourself, since we will build on the strategy foundations from the last fifty years. I aim to tie multiple ideas together into a coherent framework that keeps the focus squarely on the competitor. I will not simplify advice to "here are the moves you can make to win each and every time." No one can possibly come up with strategic guidance that works in each and every situation because different strategic questions in different sectors, in different countries, require different choices. What we will develop is a mindset, not a plug-and-play tool.

Throughout this book, I will share multiple examples to demonstrate that competitive insight is not a one-size-fits-all exercise. Please note that every company named in this text is one I have *not* worked with (at least on the particular issue discussed). All the information about these companies is based on publicly available information. For those companies I have had the opportunity to work with, I have anonymized their name or referred to them simply by the industry in which they operate.

With all the examples, and in particular the outside-in ones, I will not add any follow-up to explain why the companies acted the way they did. Part of what makes competitive insight so challenging is that you cannot ask your competitors why they did something or why they will in the future, so you will never have perfect knowledge. The point of competitive insight is not to explain why a specific action occurred in the past but to get a better understanding of what might happen in the future. Strategic thinking is inherently a forward-looking effort. The only reason you want to explain the past is as a potential predictor of the future, but as with investing, the past isn't always indicative of future performance.

Take price changes as an example. A competitor might lower prices because they are losing market share, they want to gain a specific national account, the sales force needs to hit their commission quotas, or because industry analysts all say they need to. If we looked back at one historical incident and determined it was because they were trying to win a national account, then we'd be foolish to assume the only reason they'd ever lower prices in the future was to win a new national account. You need to explore all the possible reasons why they could be lowering prices to anticipate whether any (or multiple) factors are currently pointing to an imminent decrease.

I don't want you distracted by revisionist explanations. We're not going to retroactively solve for the historical "why" but will focus on the forward-looking "how can we make sense without talking with them?" In the real world, you have to rely on second- or third-hand reporting and piece it together without the inside story.

What I have increasingly realized is that competitors are not irrational. They can be explained, but it isn't as simple as plugging data into
an algorithm. It bears repeating that competitive insight is a mindset,
not a tool. By being smart about how your organization integrates the
competitive insight activities we'll cover into your strategy development, you'll be able to ensure you won't irrationally think all of your
competitors are, well, irrational.

I Through the Looking Glass

Introduction: Companies Do the Darndest Things

In October 2019, Domino Pizza's CEO Ritch Allison appeared on CNBC's *Mad Money* to discuss his business and in particular how the delivery portion was facing increased competition from delivery apps.[1] The company had recently reduced their long-term sales guidance because more restaurants were using providers like UberEats and Postmates to deliver food. This service did not require the restaurants to invest in their own delivery system, as Domino's had over the years, thereby lowering the barrier to entry for those other restaurants to get into the food delivery sector. Allison said, "We do think there's some irrational pricing out there in the [delivery] marketplace right now funded by venture capital. . . . We don't know how long that'll last, but as we look out over the next two to three years, at the revised guidance that we've given, we've got a terrific business model."

Was it irrational for UberEats and Postmates, and the venture capitalists funding them, to invest so heavily in customer acquisition through low pricing? In hindsight, of course it wasn't since the coronavirus pandemic supercharged the transition to home food delivery. But even at the time, six months before the start of the pandemic, it still was not "irrational." Uber was investing in food delivery to keep their drivers busy enough to stay with the company (and to differentiate themselves from Lyft). Other start-ups also saw this as an opportunity consumers valued. It was rational for both players to invest to acquire customers with low delivery fees because if they didn't, then the other delivery providers would win. By acquiring customers early, before the market had settled out, the delivery apps were hoping to lock in customers (and restaurants) for the longer term, which could allow them to recoup their initial investment through higher fees in the future.

But from Domino's perspective, this investment was eating into their share of the pie. The competition was not good for them, as evidenced by the revised sales guidance to their investors. They did not want the apps slashing delivery fees because they would either have to match, which would eat into their profits, or accept losing sales to other restaurants. But that doesn't mean it was irrational.

This example illustrates two reasons why it's hard to predict competitors. First, we tend to chalk up competitor moves we don't like as irrational. If it's a move we would not make (Domino's would not have proactively slashed prices to deliver their own pizzas) or that hurts us (as UberEats and Postmates were doing to Domino's, along with competitors like DoorDash and Grubhub, with their low delivery fees), we also tend to refer to it as irrational.

The second reason it's harder to predict competitors is the changing nature of competition. Yes, every few years there's a new trend that disrupts business, but the two interconnected forces I'd like to focus on are digitization (e.g., big data, artificial intelligence, machine learning) and the way in which competitors come from other sectors and startups with greater frequency. Platformization—turning the business value chain into an ecosystem that ties together various entities—means your current competitors could create completely new value delivery systems or that your supplier could also become your competitor. Facebook has hosted news organizations' content, but they also curate and create their own users' stories, which compete with the traditional media companies for eyeballs. All four of the delivery app providers listed above are competing to ensure their platform is the one that ties together restaurants, consumers, and others (e.g., caterers, grocers) in the food ecosystem.

I've heard business leaders says things similar to Ritch Allison:

- "We have no idea what they will do because they're irrational."
- "We don't need to worry about what they'll do—they're irrational, so there's no way of knowing."
- "It would be a lot easier if everyone just acted rationally!"

If I had a nickel for every time I heard an executive utter something along these lines, I wouldn't need to be writing this book—I'd be retired on a South Pacific island. But is it just me? Was I unlucky to have worked with business leaders who view competitors as irrational? I've heard this too often: business leaders don't really say (or think) their competitors are irrational.

To find out, I conducted a survey with two simple questions: how often do your competitors act irrationally and how often do they surprise you?[2] What I found was that between 4 and 14 percent of the survey participants indicated their competitors *never* behaved irrationally across thirteen different types of strategic decisions, as seen in figure I.1.[3] The other 86–96 percent of participants believed their competitors acted irrationally at least part of the time. Half of the respondents estimated their competitors were irrational at least 26 to 50 percent of the time. (Only five participants indicated 0 percent across all thirteen categories, while one individual indicated their

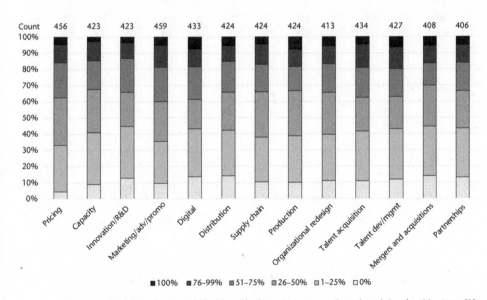

The count excludes those who answered "don't know" for that strategic category; the total population of participants was 519.

Figure I.1

Percentage of respondents indicating frequency of competitors acting *irrationally* competitors act irrationally 100 percent of the time in everything they do.)

The other question was how often competitors act surprisingly. I included the same thirteen categories, with the same percentage frequencies. As seen in figure I.2, the distribution looks very similar, but it's not a perfect overlap. Of the thirteen categories, the respondents indicated the same percentage range as they had for the irrationality question for approximately four of their answers.[4] However, the responses did not indicate a complete randomization of answers. On average, only three times (out of thirteen strategic choices) did the participants select responses for the same strategic move across the two questions that were more than one percentage range apart (e.g., they selected 1–25 percent for irrationality but 51–75 percent for being surprised, or they selected a percentage range for irrationality and "don't know" for being surprised).

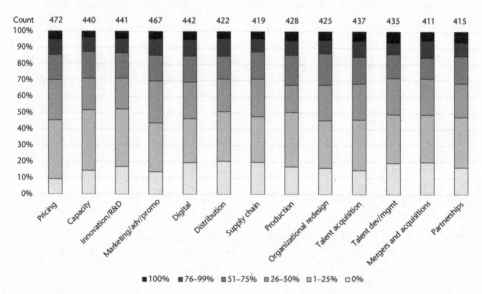

The count excludes those who answered "don't know" for that strategic category; the total population of participants was 519.

Figure I.2

Percentage of respondents indicating frequency of competitors *surprising* them

It's not unusual for business leaders to think their competitors are irrational or that they surprise them. In fact, I often sense an overlap between the two that is supported by the survey results: when competitors act surprisingly, it's often because it's a move you would not have done yourself or something you had contemplated they might do but decided they wouldn't. When I hear a business leader claim their competitor is irrational, I usually respond by asking, "Are they gaining market share? Are they profitable?" When I receive affirmative answers (and I usually do to at least one of the two questions), I ask, "Then why is it irrational to gain share and make money?" That usually leads to a pause.

But competitors are irrational, right? Even if the outcome turns out well, can't the decision itself have been irrational? Didn't they just get lucky? What we'll see is that choices that appear irrational from our perspective are often perfectly rational when viewed from the perspective of the decision maker, with the information they have at hand and the objective they are trying to achieve.

To help frame this alternative way of thinking about whether there are truly irrational decision makers, let's look at some prototypical examples of irrational choices. These are the types of strategic moves I've often seen referred to as "irrational" by those outside the organization that made them. See if you can spot your competitors' similar moves in them. After we review these examples, we'll dive a bit deeper to see how, from the outside in, we can put more perspective on them to explain why the actions were likely taken.

Irrational Is as Irrational Does

Some of these examples will be well known, but let's review them to make sure we're on the same page.

Acting Irrationally on Purpose?
A small banker in the US South had a couple of branches throughout the state, which were profitable. However, periodically, the local banker

would lower his loan rates to near his cost of capital, raise deposit rates to almost the borrowing rate, and generally set prices that drove his profits down to near zero. Why did he do this? Wasn't it irrational to lose profits by pricing so aggressively? And wasn't it irrational to do it at seemingly "random" times?

Looking in the Mirror

I was advising a transportation/logistics company [let's call them ShipCo] on the competitive pressures in their industry and how to think about optimal strategic moves to make within their network as the industry evolved: what kind of, and how many, vehicles to have in the future, routes in which to focus growing share, how pricing could be used with different customer groups, and so on.[5] We were setting up a war game simulation, and one of the client team members asked whether or not the game should include changes to warehousing capacity. The lead client team member immediately said "no" since the primary competitor was irrational with their warehousing decisions. The market was not growing, it had excess capacity, and yet this primary competitor had added four warehousing assets in the past eighteen to twenty-four months. Why would they be adding warehousing capacity if there was already enough to service the entire market? If they were that irrational, the thinking went, how could ShipCo ever possibly understand how the competitor would use warehousing assets in the future?

The competitor was like ShipCo in so many ways—covered much of the same geographical area, with similar market share and service portfolio—that it seemed obvious that they should be acting like ShipCo. And when they didn't, it must be because they were irrational.

Purposefully Destroying Value

In July 2006, NTL, a British cable provider, acquired Virgin Mobile from Sir Richard Branson, who became the largest shareholder of the combined company. The goal was to complete the vaunted quadruple play in telecommunications: landline, television, broadband internet, and cellular. Later that fall, the new Virgin Media company decided to make a bid for ITV, an independent cable television producer and broadcaster in the United Kingdom. The goal was to target ITV's landline households with the new mobile offering as well as to get existing Virgin Mobile subscribers to sign up for the landline business using ITV's existing infrastructure, which did not overlap with NTL's.

In November 2006, BSkyB, a satellite television provider owned and operated by News Corp, Rupert Murdoch's international media conglomerate, acquired a 17.9 percent stake in ITV. This gave BSkyB the ability to veto any proposed acquisition proposal, which they promptly did. Estimates at the time indicated that BSkyB had spent about 2 percent of their market capitalization to acquire the ITV stake, in addition to the lost profit they would have made from the acquisition premium Virgin Media was willing to pay. What's more irrational than wasting 2 percent of your company's value on an investment that had no immediate payoff?

Midas Touch, or Out of Touch?

General Motors (GM) introduced their built-from-the-ground-up, fully electric vehicle, the EV1, in California in 1996, partially in response to new California regulations requiring automobile manufacturers to produce zero-emission cars in their fleets. However, they stopped producing the EV1 in 1999 (producing a few more than one thousand in total) and gave up leasing them to new customers in 2002. That was five years after Toyota introduced the hybrid Prius in Japan (1997) and three years after Honda introduced their Insight hybrid vehicle in the United States (1999, a few months before the Prius entered the United States in 2000). It appeared the hybrid was going to be the environmentally friendly automobile technology of the future.

While the (very) few consumers who were able to lease the EV1 were highly favorable to the car, GM was concerned the vehicles would never develop a large enough market share. This was primarily because the price was so much higher than for an internal combustion engine automobile and because electric vehicles couldn't go very far on a single charge (the maximum range for the EV1 was no more than 140 miles across all the battery configurations). In addition, the lack of charging stations meant it would be difficult for drivers to use the EV1 as their primary mode of transportation.

But in 2003, the year after GM took the final EV1 away from customers (ultimately crushing many of them and permanently deactivating the rest), Tesla Motors was founded. Hybrid vehicles were continuing to grow their share of the automobile market, but there were fewer than fifty thousand sold in the United States in that year, hardly a resounding signal that the market was about to turn. Electric vehicles were more expensive to produce and purchase, and were less functional than hybrid vehicles, and no one had started a large-scale automobile company in decades. Why would the founders of Tesla choose to start an all-electric car company at that point in time?

Being "Little Brother"

Several years ago, a large building materials company in the construction industry was struggling to understand why a smaller player in the market was continuing to add capacity. It was a mature industry in which the large company was the market share leader. The overcapacity in the industry caused by the smaller player's additions and the downward pressure it was putting on pricing was troubling to the large player. The larger firm was befuddled: it was irrational for someone to be adding capacity in a mature market that had excess capacity! Did the smaller company just not understand how to operate in an industry with large fixed, capital costs? And what made it worse was that the start-up was founded by former employees from the existing big players in the industry, so they clearly knew how the industry should work!

Falling Victim of Circumstance?

Pepsi had long been the leading soft drink manufacturer in Thailand, one of the few countries where they could consistently outsell Coca-Cola. But in early 2013, they lost their market share lead to Coke and came in fourth behind a new start-up, est, a locally produced cola drink launched at the end of 2012, and Big Cola, a Colombian soft drink maker's product. How was est, with only a few months of sales, able to beat Pepsi, the market leader, and how did Pepsi take their eye off one of their most successful countries? Thailand has the largest per capita consumption of carbonated soft drinks in Southeast Asia, so est should not have been flying under the radar of Pepsi management watching out for new entrants (regardless of their size).

Upon Further Review . . .

Part of being a good strategist involves understanding the competition (and other stakeholders), and that requires looking at the situation from the constraints the other competitors face. Let's revisit these stories and add a bit more context to them. As we do, I'll point out that each example highlights insights I will discuss in each subsequent chapter of the book.

Acting Irrational on Purpose?

Early on, the Southern banker drew the attention of the major national banks. A few tried to enter into the regions where he was located, figuring that their lower overhead cost structure would lead to quick market share gains and profits. They priced their products when they entered at a level at which they knew the incumbent would still be able to generate profits even if they stole some of his market share. However, this was when the banker would suddenly lower his lending rates and raise his deposit rates, driving his profitability—and the potential profits for the national banks—close to zero. Inevitably, the national banks would close up shop and leave the region.

After a few attempted entries, the national banks stayed out of the territory for quite a few years. This was a perfectly rational move by the local banker to maintain his local monopoly for as long as possible. But it was described as "irrational" by the big national banks that couldn't get a foothold. Weren't they pricing so that the local banker didn't have to destroy his profitability? Weren't they pricing so as to *not* take all his market share away? Didn't he see that they could all coexist in the market?

Often, we project onto our competitors the actions we *want* them to take (such as not purposefully engaging in a price war we don't want). These desired actions are the ones that would be best for us, helping our organization to perform better. When the competitors don't oblige, we chalk their behavior up to being irrational. However, if we take the time to look at the industry from the competitor's point of view and consider their existing assets and resources (like their inability to expand nationally to compete with the larger banks), we often see that their actions *are* rational: they maximize the competitor's performance.

Looking in the Mirror

The transportation/logistics company's major competitor, the one that was adding four warehouses in the past two years, certainly seemed irrational. If they were a large, established player in a sector that wasn't growing, they should have known there was no reason to add more capacity to the market. This isn't an example of a smaller player stealing share as it grows—this was an existing market leader that wasn't going to be able to steal share and grow rapidly.

When the lead client described the competitor as "irrational," however, my ears perked up. I replied, "You're right. That does seem irrational." I paused. "Out of curiosity, how many new warehouses have you added in the last two years?"

The client looked at me quizzically. "What do you mean?"

"Just wondering if you have made any changes to your warehousing in the same time period. Have you been decreasing your warehousing space to rationalize the industry capacity?"

"No," came the answer. And then, "We've added a new warehouse in Phoenix [all city names have been changed to protect the client's identity], expanded the facility in Philadelphia, we added two new facilities in the Atlanta area, plus another one in Nashville." He paused, and asked another teammate, "Did we expand the facility in Colorado Springs?"

"No," came the reply. "We added a whole new one."

In all, the client had added or expanded at least a dozen warehousing facilities in the same time period as the competitor's four. I summarized these numbers for the lead client and asked, "So, if you were sitting in their headquarters right now, what would you think about ShipCo adding twelve new assets?"

"That ShipCo is irrational." He paused and added, "But there are good reasons why we've added or expanded those twelve sites!"

I didn't disagree. I did, however, point out that the competitor was being rather restrained in only adding one-third the number of assets as ShipCo and that they likely had a very good reason for their additions—even if that reason was to try to keep up with ShipCo.!

In chapters 1 and 2, we will delve into how to be structured and systematic when looking at the world through a competitor's eyes.

Purposefully Destroying Value

When BSkyB rejected the NTL bid for ITV, Sir Richard Branson immediately cried foul. He claimed it was "a blatant attempt to distort competition even further by blocking any attempt to create a strong and meaningful competitor."[6] But Merrill Lynch had estimated that BSkyB was destroying 2 percent of their market cap to "prevent [their] largest competitor [NTL] potentially buying a company [ITV] which could have given the cable operator some competitive advantage in the future. This seems like a reasonable price to pay."[7] It was perfectly rational for BSkyB to have bought a controlling interest to block the acquisition. But how could Virgin Media have known this?

First of all, Branson had been part of the consortium that had won the government bid for the British satellite broadcasting license in the mid-1980s, only to see Rupert Murdoch's News Corp preempt them by launching Sky TV in the United Kingdom. News Corp used a satellite orbiting over Spain, which was exempt from British control. So Branson had experienced Rupert Murdoch's finding ways to change the game in order to win. (BSkyB was actually the merger between Sky TV and British Satellite Broadcasting, which won the original government license.)

But that was almost twenty years prior, so maybe he shouldn't have been expected to remember. Except in October 2006, Rupert Murdoch's Australian newspaper, the *Daily Telegraph*, had purchased a 7.5 percent

stake in the *Sydney Morning Herald*. When asked why, Murdoch stated
it was "just to make it difficult for anybody to take them over" and
that they "could increase the stake to 10 per cent if a rival bidder came
along."[8] In other words, News Corp had employed the same strategy
one month prior to the NTL-ITV episode!

Viewing the world through Murdoch's eyes can be supplemented
by a structured way of thinking about how a competitor will react to
your specific moves, which we will cover in chapter 3. While we cannot
guarantee that using these insights would have predicted Murdoch's
purchase of the ITV shares, it is *much* more likely that Virgin Media
could have foreseen the potential reaction and structured the bid to
minimize the chance of a blocking bid at the last moment.

Midas Touch, or Out of Touch?

Tesla's first vehicle was the Roadster sports car, priced over $100,000.
It had serious power under the hood: it went from zero to sixty in less
than four seconds. By contrast, the EV1 took eight seconds to get up to
that speed. The Roadster was *sold* to high-end buyers, whereas the EV1
had been *leased* to drivers, at an implied price of $34,000. The high-
end sticker price for the Roadster conveyed a similar sense of high-end
status to those who drove them. And contrary to the EV1, the Roadster
could go almost 250 miles on a single charge.

At the time GM canceled the EV1, there were long waitlists for leases
on the vehicle, which was evidence that consumers *did* want to acquire
electric vehicles. But Tesla didn't rush to satisfy the demand from that
particular market segment. They took five years between the launch
of the company and the first car delivery to work out some of the initial design kinks. They contracted out with Lotus to build the chassis
for them, which allowed them to focus on the battery and motor that
would power the vehicle.

After the contract with Lotus ended, Tesla moved on to the Model
S sedan, which was first sold in 2012. This replaced production of the
Roadster but kept a premium price tag starting at $57,400 and running
up to $87,400. By the end of the year, there were reservations for fifteen

thousand of the cars. As we know today, Tesla is one of the most valuable automobile companies in the world, and they continue to be a leader in the electric vehicle space.

How did they succeed? Tesla attacked the market from the top instead of from the bottom. They sold high-end cars that helped provide them with extra financial cushion (they were still losing money early on but they would have lost even more if they sold cars at a lower price). They also were paying attention to the successes (and failures) in the EV1 program. In 2017, Elon Musk, the chairman and CEO of Tesla, tweeted that "we started Tesla when GM forcibly recalled all electric cars from customers in 2003 & then crushed them in a junkyard."[9]

Could the other incumbent car companies have foreseen Tesla? They all observed GM's experiment with EV1. While they were mostly focusing on hybrid engine technology at that time, there were five years when Tesla was developing the Roadster in which they could have learned about it (Tesla contracted out with BorgWarner, a large supplier to the existing manufacturers, in addition to their work with Lotus). And Musk was a serial entrepreneur who had been disrupting other industries in his previous ventures.

In chapter 4, we'll explore how to predict those spontaneous moves that current or future competitors make unexpectedly, gaining better foresight on when those moves might occur, and in what form. And in chapter 5, I'll provide insights from other professionals who have similar challenges. Companies can't directly ask their competitors what they plan to do or why they made past decisions. Antitrust laws in most jurisdictions rule that out. But homicide detectives, neonatal intensive care unit (NICU) nurses, paleontologists, and archaeologists all face the same constraints. Interviews with over two dozen of these professionals have led to best practice tips and tricks that have been synthesized for business leaders.

Being "Little Brother"

The building materials company asked for our help to design, build, and facilitate a war game to understand the pricing and capacity dynamics in the industry. During the game, the team playing the small upstart added capacity round after round, and they ended up with the greatest market share gains and profit levels in each period. The client, and the other larger incumbents in the exercise, continued to lose share, while their profits eroded due to their attempts at preventing further share losses through price decreases. This continued until the last round, in which the upstart team no longer had the largest share gain or profit levels.

Those of us running the workshop noticed the smaller team had not added capacity in the final round, which surprised us since it had been a winning formula to that point. In the debrief session conducted immediately upon finishing the game, we asked the upstart team why they had failed to add capacity in the last round. The response was that "we started to think like ourselves [i.e., the client's view of the world that adding capacity was a bad idea], so we didn't increase our output." We then informed them that had they indeed added capacity in line with the previous rounds, they would again have won greater share gains and profit levels.

We asked the team role-playing the upstart to explain why they chose to add capacity in every round (except the final one), and they explained that from the financial projections for their company, adding capacity made sense. They didn't care that the larger players were losing share and had excess capacity. The company they were role-playing was capacity constrained and needed to add capacity each round. This explanation was so simple. The rest of the participants immediately realized the reason the smaller player's moves seemed irrational was because they weren't viewing the market through the perspective of that company but through the client's lens. Seen from the vantage of the upstart, though, they all agreed that they too would have added capacity.

While this asymmetry is often most obvious when confronting competitors of a different size, the same principles apply to any type of asymmetry: different resources, relationships, knowledge, or competencies. We need to view the world from the perspective of having those different "toys to play with" and mindsets for using them.

War games are fantastic exercises for uncovering why competitors behave the way they do. The effort forces participants to not only think about the other players but also act on their behalf. This heightened involvement leads to a deeper understanding beyond merely reading reports and contemplating them. (Which is still better than nothing!)

War game workshops also allow for creative strategy development. Stepping outside the day-to-day grind is enhanced by experiencing the market through another company's viewpoint. The shackles that bind participants to "how we usually do things" are suddenly removed, and the freedom unleashes creativity that is applicable—the players are trying to win the game, not just come up with creative ideas. One of the outcomes of a workshop is a list of all the moves the competitor teams developed during the exercise. For those that were successful in the game, the obvious question is "Can we do that first?"

Finally, competitive insight exercises are great for team building and alignment. If a small team develops the competitive insight in closed-door meetings, the results may not be broadly accepted by the rest of the leadership team. But if the whole team is actively participating in developing the insights, there is a shared understanding and language. I've had clients who for years afterward refer to the war games we ran together as they continue to discuss the future of their industry and strategy. That shared memory is hard to build otherwise.

In chapter 6, I'll explain what war games are and how to conduct them (and other exercises to gain competitive insight) so you can better prepare and practice your strategic moves before confronting the challenges of the real world.

Falling Victim of Circumstance?

Viewed from the outside, it appears that Pepsi had faced several organizational alignment issues with their Thai operations. For example, they had tried, and failed, to acquire their Thai distributor, Sermsuk, in 2010. Sermsuk and Pepsi agreed in 2011 to end their almost sixty-year exclusive distribution contract in November 2012, when the latest contract was set to expire. The contract's noncompete clause happened to expire the same day as the distribution contract, so Sermsuk was able to immediately begin selling est—their own cola product—the very next day. Sermsuk had been preparing to respond to the end of the deal for almost two years, so they were ready for the contract's expiration. Pepsi had built a $170 million bottling plant in Thailand to be ready to supply the market, but they were still working on getting enough distribution assets in place to get the bottles to retailers (DHL, Pepsi's distribution partner, had the capability to supply larger retailers but not the bulk of the smaller Thai store owners). In addition, Pepsi switched their packaging from glass to plastic even though Thai consumers prefer glass bottles.

While these could be chalked up to execution errors, we can also ask whether the right information was shared throughout the Pepsi organization on the competitive threats to their Thai market leadership. Reports indicate the company had recently experienced a large turnover in brand managers throughout the organization (though it is unclear if this directly affected the Thai Pepsi brand managers), so the bench strength of knowledge was challenged. Also, in hindsight it's clear that the following groups needed to have a deep sharing of information:

- lawyers who managed the contract and noncompete clauses
- operations folks who would know about Sermsuk's ability to begin producing and selling their own cola product
- operations personnel who were responsible for the interaction with DHL and the production capabilities of the new Pepsi bottling plant
- marketers who understood the threats Coca-Cola could make (based on their recent gains in market share)
- marketers who understood the consumer preferences for different bottle materials
- operations staff who could relay rumors they heard from bottling material suppliers on what others were using or experimenting with
- division leaders who had to coordinate all the various pieces of information

That's a lot of disparate information floating around the company, all pertaining *only* to the Thai cola business!

How do you make sure all of that data is shared, analyzed, and made actionable? A well-functioning competitive insight team helps in these situations. It doesn't matter if the competitor—or potential competitor—is big or small. What matters is that your organization can share the appropriate information to develop the competitive insight. I'll describe in chapter 7 what a competitive insight function does and how to integrate it with the rest of the organization.

Why Should You Care about Your Competitors?

I've been assuming that you already are convinced that you must be focused on your competitors and their actions. In some sense, the fact that you are reading this is validation enough. But before we dive in further, let's step back and highlight why a better understanding of competitors is a crucial capability that all strategists should possess.

Competitor Decisions Will Often Affect Your Business Outcomes

The most obvious reason you should care about understanding your competitors is that, almost certainly, they will affect your organization's performance. There are very few industries where the actions of any one firm in the sector have no noticeable impact on the actions of the others. In reality, there are always individual competitors that every company focuses on—either as a potential roadblock or an aspirational target. They are the ones we focus on precisely because they influence the success of our own organizations. Instead of dreading those competitors, let's learn how to better understand them so they are less likely to surprise you with their actions.

New Competitors Can Emerge from Anywhere

How business strategists think of industries is shifting from a value chain perspective, where upstream suppliers sell to downstream producers who then sell to customers, to an ecosystem perspective. The latter includes suppliers and customers but is less linear: suppliers can also be customers, suppliers can be competitors in subsectors (or other industries), and complementors can become suppliers, customers, or competitors. The product or service you offer can now be a platform upon which other ecosystem partners build their businesses and help sustain yours through the platform. The automotive sector—a traditional value chain industry for much of the twentieth century—is now becoming an ecosystem, with the vehicle as the platform tying together various content and innovation partners. Legacy automobile manufacturers are wrestling whether to sell directly to consumers who order electric vehicles online or through the dealers. The dealers' former suppliers could become their biggest competitors.

Everyone—Even a Monopolist—Has Competitors

All companies have competitors, whether they are for-profit or nonprofit, publicly traded or privately held, whether they are monopolists or operate in a highly competitive industry, or whether they are established companies or innovative start-ups. Nonprofit companies must compete with for-profit companies if they offer similar products and services. Monopolists (like utilities) sell to customers who have alternatives (like distributed power generation, or using electricity instead of natural gas, or cutting the cable TV cord for mobile- or internet-based video). Philanthropic organizations compete with other charitable groups for limited donor funding. And innovative entrepreneurs, who feel they have developed a brand-new service, are still competing with others who are providing a comparable service in a different manner (potentially less efficiently but still being provided—e.g., Uber competes with taxi cabs, Airbnb competes with hotels and motels, and even the iPhone was competing with flip phones, the PalmPilot, GPS-only devices, and netbooks when initially introduced).

So even if you think you don't have competitors—you do! Resources are limited and consumer mindsets are not infinite, so there will always be constraints imposed by others that affect you. If you mistake the competitive response, you're likely to run into a brick wall, not an open path to success. If you know where the wall is, you can go around, over, or under it and arrive unscathed at the other side.

The Techniques in This Book Are Broadly Applicable

Even if you *still* don't think that you have to worry about competitors, there is always someone else you need to understand. The frameworks and techniques explained in this book will also work on complementors (those who help your company along the way), partners, other stakeholders (like unions or activist investors or nongovernmental organizations), regulators, and anyone else who impacts your organization.

And these frameworks and ideas also apply to understanding individuals within your organization (other colleagues you work with, direct reports you have to manage, the bosses you need to maneuver through) as well as people in your everyday life. I am not suggesting that you need to war game your way through discussing whether to buy a new house with your partner, but the mindset of thinking about the other person's viewpoint, as well as their constraints and decision-making process, is just as relevant for our personal interactions as for when we are at work.

So even if you are not quite convinced that you have competitors you need to worry about, or if you work for a nongovernmental or governmental organization, you will still be better able to improve your empathy skills toward others you interact with, and that's valuable for all leaders.

Are They Irrational?

Now that I've (hopefully) convinced you that the rest of the book is applicable to you, regardless of your organization, let's return to the question of whether competitors act irrationally. All of the stories detailed above have a common theme: viewed from the outside, the decisions look "irrational." I believe this word is thrown around a bit too loosely. Behavioral economists use the term in a very specific manner. The assumptions underlying much of economic thinking assumes a certain type of "rational" behavior, and behavioralists point out all the ways humans' actual behavior doesn't match those prescriptive norms. Behavioral economists aren't wrong: far be it from me to contradict one of the biggest improvements to economic thinking in the last few decades, one with which I wholeheartedly agree! However, in practice, the terminology's usage focuses less on this theoretical basis and instead on what we've discussed above: their choices don't make sense or are surprising, partly because they are not what we would do (or what we would want them to do). This viewpoint creates another set of biases that prevent us from truly empathizing when interacting with others.

I want you to stop using "irrational" when you really mean "surprising" or "confusing" and instead think of truly irrational behavior as that which is not in their own best interests (i.e., they're making choices they know are harmful to them) or is completely random and has no connection to the facts in the case (i.e., throwing a dart at the world map while blindfolded to determine an international expansion strategy). I consider this latter category irrational (while others might not) because there is always value in trying to collect some data and analyzing it. You may not get the right data, or the right conclusions, but at least you are trying, and that's better than making random decisions.

Upon closer inspection, in all of the examples described above, the organizational leaders were making choices that looked irrational through your eyes but if viewed from their perspective suddenly make a lot of sense. My contention is that this is the predominant set of "irrational" moves—they are not truly irrational but can be explained clearly and rationally once viewed from the decision maker's perspective. They are predictable.[10] We often mistakenly think our competitors (and other stakeholders) are making irrational choices because we're imposing our frame of reference, our fact base, our timeframe, and our analytic technique to their problems. Or we are being biased by forgetting that others are subject to common decision-making biases! But if we use their frame, available facts, timing, and techniques, their choices become clearer.

This doesn't mean that everything can be justified as rational. Using the same set of facts, what might be rational in the short term might not be rational in the long term. What may be rational with a goal of maximizing market share won't always support maximizing profit margins (though it could possibly maximize total profits).

My colleague Peter Boumgarden suggested an interesting thought experiment to try to help clarify this: "What would the world look like if you walked through it thinking everyone was irrational? Now imagine that you changed your perspective and viewed everyone as making purely rational decisions. How would that change your outlook?" I clearly fall in the latter camp: everyone is rational, but they have different endowments, preferences, objectives, histories, and risk profiles, which implies that we should all be making different choices. If we assume everyone is irrational, it leads to a cessation of trying to figure them out (since they're irrational!), which is dangerous. We would be walking around randomly changing our paths—while walking on the street, interacting in relationships, or planning for the future—because we believe the stimuli from others are also going to be random (and unpredictable). Or we'd react to those random inputs by putting our heads down and plowing forward; crossing our fingers that luck will keep others out of our way or prevent bad things from happening. Neither is a very pleasant way to live.

Instead, I'd prefer to engage with my surroundings by assuming that others have a purpose in life—I just need to figure out what those goals and rationales are. I would try to assess how best to achieve those things that I want out of life by determining the best way to get the necessary help from others—or avoid the obstacles they put in my way. I would nurture relationships to create win-win outcomes and stronger bonds throughout my community and the broader society. That's the recipe for a life well lived.

The rest of this book will help you understand how to think like the competitor, how to embed these ideas into practical applications, and how to redesign your organization to ensure these techniques are used. The world is a crazy place, but often you are the root cause: you are irrationally assuming that the rest of the world is just like you. Open your eyes, engage with the world, and recognize that we're not all the same. Appreciate the diversity in the world so you can carve out your own unique path.

II Your Irrational Competitor

1 How Can You Get inside Your Competitor's Head?

High-level team sports require each side to be ruthless about preparation and internal focus. Players and coaches must drill constantly to perfect specific plays so they can be executed during the games. However, each team cannot just concentrate on their own performance: they also need to pay attention to their future opponent. They need to track what the opponent has done in the past and where they have excelled and where they are vulnerable. They need to analyze how the other side is positioned for the upcoming game and whether there are personnel changes that will influence the opponent's strategy. And then they need to make predictions about the plays the adversary might run so they can select the best ones to hone from their own arsenal in preparation for the upcoming contest.

Sports teams have developed methods to help them gain insight into their competitors. These include the following:

- sending scouts to observe the other team's games
- watching voluminous amounts of film of the other team's games
- listening to the opponent's press conferences and reading articles about them
- debriefing their own players and coaches who used to play or work for the opponent
- tracking the opponent's statements on player injuries
- observing changes in the opponent's personnel—both players and coaches (including who was promoted from within the organization)

By compiling this information, a head coach can understand the competitor from their past actions (from game film or direct observation), identify the changes they have made within their team, assess whether the loss (or return from injury) of specific players could affect the opponent's ability to execute a game plan, and update the likely game strategies based on which coaches will be working on the field on game day.

Pulling together these predictions allows a head coach to prepare their own team's game plan. The best coaches don't stop there: they continually assess how the current game is unfolding with particular attention to any changes the opponent is making that weren't planned for originally. At breaks in the game (half time, time outs, etc.), these managers will modify their strategy if they think their original game plan no longer meets the reality of that day's contest.

Smart businesspeople follow a similar plan to understand and out-compete their competitors. They think about what their competitors have said and done, what resources they have added (or assets they have lost), and any leadership changes they have made. They combine all of this information with a real-time view of the situation to update their insight over time.

Understanding the competition involves these four steps:

1. Review public communication and actions.
2. Assess competitor assets and resources.
3. Consider the human factor.
4. Predict, observe, and adjust.

In this chapter, I'll highlight how these four steps relate to the business environment and how to tie them together into a coherent process for getting inside the head of your competitor.[1] Sure, it's fun to think about competitors in the context of sports, but it's more important to know how to apply this to your competitor in a multimillion-dollar market. Just as teams can get into serious trouble with their leagues for not following the rules (like the New England Patriots football team did when they videotaped an opponent's practice), my advice here is not to spy on your competitors and use questionable (or illegal) methods for gathering information on them. Instead, a savvy, competition-aware businessperson will use all the legal means at their disposable to collect data, facts, and information about competitors and then synthesize it into a coherent prediction about their competitor's mindset.

Step 1: Review Public Communication and Actions

The first step of competitive insight involves what most people think of as competitive intelligence: paying attention to what the competitors say and do. At this stage, a litany of sources come into play: annual reports, earnings conference calls, speeches by company leaders, company press releases, booths or presentations from industry conferences, and press articles.

The information within these sources is a great first step to building an understanding of the competitor, but it cannot remain just a collection of documents that sits on the shelf (or on a shared drive in the cloud). First, you have to read the information and then connect and compare the different strands within it. At a minimum, you have to determine whether the competitor is consistent in their public statements. Is the CEO saying that they are looking at expanding into Indonesia, while the head of Asia-Pacific is talking instead about Vietnam? Are their researchers who speak at industry conferences talking about oncology medications while their press releases tout clinical trials in cardiovascular drugs?

If the competitor is consistent in what they are saying across various levels of their organization, then you should have good confidence that what they say is what they are focusing on doing. It's true that it could be a huge ruse to throw you and fellow competitors off their trail, but it would take an extremely disciplined organization to be that consistently on-message across a large number of people without some conflicting messages leaking through. On the other hand, if individuals at the competitor are all saying different things, then you should question whether they are internally confused (which could be good for you if it

slows them down from making decisions) or whether they are purposefully trying to mislead you. This is where the second element of "what
they say" comes into play: how they say it.

It is important to pay attention to intonation, emphasis, context,
and all the other nonverbal factors within the competitor's communications. The same words can convey different intent depending on the
way sounds are made. Take the word "right" as an example. You can
say it sarcastically, emphatically, questioningly, encouragingly, disbe-
lievingly, threateningly, and even seductively. The same is true for a
statement from a business leader on a conference call. They can ignore
a question, brush it off, answer it curtly, respond with passion, ramble
on with extraneous explanation, or deflect the question and answer on
a different topic. If you are reading the response on a transcript, you
can read between the lines and ascribe intent to the words. Many times,
listening to the actual audio file of the answer helps. Did the speaker
pause often as they answered the question (those pauses—either before
the answer or embedded within it—might not make it into the tran-
scribed version), or did they plow through as quickly as possible? The
former indicates uncertainty, nervousness, or guardedness in the reply,
while the latter could be annoyance, confidence, or impatience to move
on to other topics.

The good news is that many companies upload their conference calls
to their investor websites, so you can download the audio files for publicly traded companies. For private companies, focus on presentations
the leaders make on televised news programs or in speeches that are
videotaped and uploaded to the web. The internet is a great source of
information if you dig around—but you must know what you're looking for, avoiding the temptation to surf for just anything.

You should also pay attention to what competitors have done in
the past. As I was told while growing up, "actions speak louder than
words." Explore whether there are certain patterns in the competitor's
prior choices—big moves always made at a certain time of year, changes
that often begin at a certain place or in a certain way, a tendency to
make leadership changes before undertaking a new strategy, and so on.

The competition won't always repeat past behaviors, but if there are strong patterns in the competitor's past actions, it helps paint the picture of the competitor's general mindset.

Paying attention to what competitors say sounds easy, and most companies would say they do that. But paying attention and doing it well are two different things. Be certain that you, or someone in your organization, are taking the time needed to analyze the words and how they are said. Once you know what the competitor has said (and how), you can turn to thinking about what they are capable of doing.

Step 2: Assess Competitor Assets and Resources

If a competitor has said they are planning to expand their product sales into a new country but they have no marketing staff in the country, nor any distribution assets or partnerships, it will be very hard for them to actually pull it off. At this stage, you should start looking at your competitor to assess what exactly they can bring to bear when executing their strategic plans.

I like to call this step "What toys can they play with?" What are their assets, resources, capabilities, and competencies that would allow their organization to be successful? What could they use to execute the strategies you've identified in step 1? Examples of these assets and resources include production and distribution capacity, human capital, patents, knowledge, partnerships, existing market share, financial resources, brand, reputation, geographic footprint, and internal organizational processes.

Understanding what toys the competitor has to play with is a harder task than reviewing their public communications, to be sure. You generally cannot walk into their facilities and look around. You can't talk with their HR department about their personnel processes. But even though you can't ask directly, you can still gather information about these assets and resources. For publicly traded firms, information about their financial resources, market shares, and geographic footprint is often contained in public investor disclosures (often mandated by legal requirements in different regions). Partnerships are typically announced in press releases and news articles. Brand values and rankings are estimated by independent organizations. And if the competitor is big enough, there might even be news articles written about what makes them tick.

You will find similar information in analyst reports. In particular, analysts will often opine on the competencies and capabilities they ascribe to the competitor. Just because it's in writing doesn't mean it's true nor that you should believe it. But if it fits with your organization's thoughts about what the competitor does well, then give more credence to the reports.

Mystery shopping and reverse engineering are two other techniques that can be used to gather information, especially for product-based competitors. How do they sell their product? Through which channels? How can you purchase it? What are its components? These tried-and-true methodologies should be used on new products in particular, and they can help validate whether statements from the leadership (step 1) align with the actual product on the street.

Another great tool to use here is the software you use to track your organization's reputation online. Many companies use these tools to see whether their social media content and strategies are portraying them in a favorable light. Turn that same software around and use it to assess the online reputation of your competitor. Are the recent product reviews trending in positive or negative ways? What comments and feedback are their customers leaving on retailer sites? Use text mining software to find examples where people compare your product to the competitor's and then read those reviews to learn where they have a competitive advantage. Test to see if certain keywords you feel are crucial to their success are being used by reviewers. It's true that you cannot believe everything you read on the internet, and reviews on shopping sites are not always valid. But to the extent that you use these tools to assess your own performance, you should also apply them to your competitors. You can (selectively) assess what their reputation is around the key products or services with which you compete.

There are two key principles to keep in mind. First, you need to focus on the assets and capabilities that matter in your industry. For example, in pharmaceuticals, research and development (R&D) and patents are important. For durable manufacturing, it's often capacity and supply chains. For consumer-packaged goods, brands and retail distribution channels are a good place to start. You know your industry, and you know what your competitors brag about that makes them different and special. Focus on those assets and capabilities rather than a generic off-the-shelf list.

The second principle is to pay attention to the drivers, not just the outcomes. Take patents as an example. You should absolutely keep track of all the new and existing patents your competitors have. But the patents are the end result of their R&D investment. Predicting future launches requires you to dig back and create a linkage between when a patent was awarded (or filed) and when the product based on it was launched. Use this information to predict when a new product will be launched after a future patent is granted. Ideally, however, you want awareness even before they obtain a patent. To that end, you should be tracking changes in R&D spend (broken out by division, if possible). You should also track new partnerships with academic institutions. Has the competitor hired new research staff? Are they still trying to hire (e.g., what job postings have they uploaded to job search sites, are they interviewing at academic conferences)? What backgrounds do they seek? To get the best insight on where competitors are headed, focus on the drivers of the outcomes you observe in the market.

Consider a cereal manufacturer whose market share has stayed flat, while one competitor has grown from 29 to 33 percent share, and the other has shrunk from 31 to 27 percent.[2] Which competitor should they be worried about? Should they worry about the first one since they have grown and have the largest share? The bigger one may be happy with the share they have and don't plan to grow further, while the smaller one may be freaking out because they've lost their lead and will aggressively try to regain it. Just by looking at the trends that have occurred in the past doesn't help us predict the future actions.

But if we knew the competitor that lost share had told investors they were going to refocus on that market, had increased their promotional budget, signed a deal to cobrand with Disney characters, and hired a new national accounts manager (see step 3), we would know they will aggressively try to recapture share. If they instead state they are shifting focus to a different geography, or to produce for private label sellers, or to different product categories, then we'd be less concerned about their future choices. Just looking at the current outcomes in the market isn't enough to indicate the future actions.

By paying attention to what the competitor says, and thinking about whether they have the assets and resources to actualize their goals, you will be most of the way toward thinking about the world from their viewpoint. The next step makes this personal.

Step 3: Consider the Human Factor

The first two steps could trap you into thinking of your competitor as a black box, an organization that is reduced to a set of statements and building blocks that will execute strategies on their own. As we know, however, organizations are composed of people. Individuals make the statements you hear and read in step 1. (Even if those statements are put out by the communications department, someone had to write the first draft, and someone else almost assuredly edited it, and a third person might have even had to sign off on it.)

In this third stage, you need to pay attention to the decision makers, and there are two elements that come into play here. The first is determining the history and background of the person—or group of people—who are making the decisions. In 2008, a high-tech firm was designing a war game to test how the industry might evolve. The teams were going to make choices on R&D investment, product portfolio, and pricing, among others. As we were building out the game, we started to debate whether to allow the teams to enter into partnerships with each other (or with others who were outside the scope of the game), including merging with or acquiring each other.

The client was initially reluctant—they stated that since the industry was relatively consolidated, no mergers or acquisitions would be allowed by the competition authorities in the major markets where they sold their products. On the surface, this made sense. But then I pointed out that one of their competitors (who was going to be represented by a team in the game) had just hired a new head of strategy. That new chief strategy officer (CSO) had been in charge of a large regional mergers and acquisition (M&A) practice at Goldman Sachs. The competitor did not hire this person to come up with a better marketing strategy.

This is a crucial insight when viewing the leadership—and especially leadership changes—at your competitor. As with overall organizational history, past behavior isn't a perfect predictor of future actions, but it's a pretty good indicator. Boards of directors hire CEOs based on the candidate's background and on the assumption that the CEO will execute similar strategies in their new role. A senior executive who came up through the ranks as a marketer won't suddenly start focusing on supply chain optimization or operational improvement efforts in the production facilities. That new executive will focus primarily on marketing in order to achieve the organization's strategic objectives.

There are two reasons to believe this assumption. First, the board hired her because of her marketing background, and second, that's what the executive knows! A marketing expert knows how to market products and services, how to think about marketing challenges, and how to execute marketing strategies. Most senior executives have to deliver—and quickly. The easiest way to accomplish that is by doing what they know best.

Is it possible that it's a misdirection on the part of the board? It's not likely. If the board had told the CEO of this plan (we want to hire you as a marketing expert but want you to focus on operational efficiency), the CEO would not have accepted: it's too big a risk. She would have been set up to fail because the job would not play to her core strengths. It's doubtful someone would accept the job *knowing* that the board was trying to mislead competitors, and on the chance the CEO did accept the job under these conditions, she would likely default to leveraging her core skills anyway. (Besides, the CEO could be in trouble with securities regulators since she would also be misleading investors. The CEO should also seriously question the board's values since they would be misleading investors too!) On the other hand, what if the board decided to keep this misdirection hidden from the CEO hire? The new CEO will choose to focus on her leadership and functional strengths anyway because she'll assume that was why the board hired her.

The good news is that it's not that difficult to find biographical information on senior executives for most organizations. Many companies post bios and responsibilities of senior executives on their websites (search for the company name and "management" or "leadership"). In addition, senior leaders at public and private companies are usually announced with great fanfare, including a rather robust bio that details all their accomplishments—and justifies why that person is a great addition to the organization's senior leadership team. Look at the news feed for your competitors and read the details on the last few senior executives who were hired or promoted. You'll quickly discover the depth of material you can gather about your competitors' leaders from these postings.

If for some reason the new hire is announced in a short one-sentence press release and the company doesn't post leadership profiles, you can always look to places like LinkedIn or a general internet search. The person's previous employer may still have a bio listed on their website, or other business information sites like Bloomberg or Hoovers could still list information on the executive from a previous role. The good news in today's internet age is that you don't need an inside source to learn about someone's background—most people post it themselves on LinkedIn, or a few minutes surfing the web can uncover relevant information.

The second element at play in this step is assessing the potential for principal-agent problems at your competitor: the incentives of the agent may not align with the incentives of the principal. A classic example is when shareholders (the principal) hire the board (the agent) to maximize their welfare and when the board (the principal) then turns around and hires a CEO (the agent) to achieve those goals. The shareholders and board want the CEO to maximize returns, while the CEO may have other ambitions. One behavioral bias that crops up is the empire building effect, where the CEO focuses on expanding the size and reach of the organization to increase his own power. These actions may sometimes be in the best interest of the corporation, but often they are not adding value to the company, just merely to the CEO.

Agency problems come into play in understanding competitors because the person you listen to may not be the one executing the decisions. If the person who implements the actual decision is not the one you are paying attention to, you could have a misleading impression of the competitor's intent. An example makes this easier to understand. Say the CEO has announced that the company is planning to raise prices by 10 percent in the coming year based on increases in the cost of materials and the need to recover some fixed costs incurred during the R&D of next-generation products. On the surface, it seems a reasonable decision. If the competitors believe the CEO, they might decide to raise their prices in conjunction (which is possibly part of the reason the first company wanted to raise prices—so others would follow and they wouldn't have to compete as aggressively on price). But the competitors should wait to see if this is a ruse by the first company: saying they will raise prices so the others follow and then keeping their prices low to gain more market share. If the competitors see the first company starting to lower prices again, they'll go back to competing heavily on price too.

In many industries, the sales force is compensated on a commission, so individual sales agents (note that word) have an incentive to sell as much as possible to reach their quota or the next level of bonus. What's the best way for an individual salesperson to close the next deal? Give a little bit back on price, especially if the customer is claiming that the competitors haven't raised their prices or that the customer just can't afford it. So the sales agent closes a big deal with a discount. The deal is big enough that the competitors will know they've lost, and they'll probably hear through their sales reps that the winning company gave a discount to secure the business. This seemingly confirms that the competitor CEO's announcement was a trick to win more share. Price competition then continues, possibly stronger than before.

We've seen this in many different industries. For example, the CEO announces to the market that the company will be raising prices to offset costs. Internally, she tells the sales agents that they shouldn't cut price to win a specific deal. If the authorization thresholds are not rigid, the salesperson must decide whether to adhere to the corporate strategy or to ignore the policy, offer a discount, win the contract, and earn a commission. The individual sales rep will often make the best choice for themselves. The message you receive is muddled: are they raising prices (like the CEO announced) or lowering them (which the customer said was the reason the competitor won the contract)?

As a competitor, you need to understand the individual incentives of the people executing the decisions. Is the sales force compensated on commission? If so, that will make price increases harder to execute. Are the researchers in R&D paid a flat salary, or are they granted bonuses for patents? Are they evaluated on the sales of the products they develop? If they are paid a straight salary, there is less incentive to crank out new ideas. Are country or regional managers compensated on their own geographical performance or on overall corporate outcomes? If the former, there will likely be different choices made in different regions. Are regional managers rotated around the company every two to three years? In that case, look for choices that boost short-term performance at the expense of longer-term outcomes. You can't perfectly know which HR policies your competitor is implementing, but by asking around—especially of others who used to work at that company (ask your legal department for the right way to do this!)—you can realize a general understanding.

Do they truly encourage dissent? Does hierarchy matter? Do decisions have to go through multiple committees or are individuals empowered to make decisions? Is there an investment amount threshold above which senior approval is needed? You can also go through your external network, or those of colleagues at your company, to see if there are members who are former employees of the competitor. Seek those individuals out to see if they have insight. (Did you ever talk or work with the specific decision maker much? Do you have any complaints about where you used to work? Anything you'd like to brag about?) Again—and I can't stress this enough—preclear these efforts with your organization's legal counsel. Different organizations have different risk preferences and tolerances for how far you can probe—don't make that assessment yourself.

We can't perfectly know the competitor's organizational dynamics and power structures, but that's not the point—you want to build an understanding of those dynamics from the outside. (After all, could you completely and accurately describe how decisions are made within your current organization? You could for your area, almost certainly, but could you do this for other divisions or functional areas? If not, how can we expect to ever have perfect understanding of another organization's dynamics?) This isn't a rules-based set of outcomes: this is about understanding whatever you can of the decision maker's incentives and then seeing if those incentives align with what you've been hearing the competitor say (step 1) and what you know about their resources and assets (step 2). As previously mentioned, the competitor is not a black box that makes decisions—instead, every organization is made up of people who make choices based on their job responsibilities and incentives. Use that knowledge to help refine your understanding of the competitor.

Step 4: Predict, Observe, and Adjust

At the end of step 3, you are now in a position to make a prediction about what the competitor is thinking and how they'll likely act in any situation. Step 4 is also about determining where you were right and where you were wrong about your prediction.

Philip Tetlock and Dan Gardner's *Superforecasting* provides a great overview of good and bad practices when making predictions, which are also applicable for predicting competitors.[3] Some of the key best practice takeaways include the following:

- *Ask specific questions*: Predictions should not be about vague generalities like "Will the competitors change prices in the future" but more specific, such as "Will Competitor X decrease prices in Western Europe by at least 5 percent before December 31?" You can ask the same question with multiple variations—different regions, different competitors, different price changes—but the more specific, the better.

- *Make short-term predictions*: Forecasting research demonstrates that no one is capable of consistently beating random guessing when making predictions out a few years or more. For competitive insight, this means you should make predictions about whether the competitor will decrease pricing in the next three months or introduce a new product in the next six months or make an acquisition before the end of the year. You shouldn't ignore longer-term questions like "Will Company Y invade our industry in the next three years?" Instead, you should break that question down into smaller increments that assess the drivers that would ultimately lead to answering that bigger question. For example, "Will Company Y hire away R&D staff from us or a competitor in the next six months?" or "Will Company Y apply for patents that could be used in our industry by the end of the year?"

- *Be curious*: Superforecasters (the best of the best) are always reading from multiple sources and seeking out new perspectives on the question at hand. Instead of returning to the same experts or media sites over and over, they purposefully seek out alternative points of view to ensure they get a well-rounded fact base upon which to make their projections. Competitive analysts should be seeking different industry analysts, reports from different geographies, media reports across the political spectrum, and generalist media sources in addition to industry publications.

- *Be comfortable with numbers*: The best forecasters must be able to apply base rate probabilities, differentiate between probabilities of as little as one percentage point, and be able to average estimates from a group of analysts. Competitive insight analysts must be able to assess the impact of a competitor's 5 percent price decrease on their profitability or market share in order to assess how likely they would be to execute the price change. Superforecasters do not build large, complex mathematical models that estimate the probability for them, but they do have a sense for when the numbers don't add up and how to view them with a critical eye.

- *Update frequently by small amounts*: Superforecasters update predictions multiple times as new information is revealed, but they rarely make large probability estimate changes. If you thought the competitor had a 62 percent chance of dropping prices by 5 percent and then heard from the sales force that a customer was asking for a similar price decrease from that competitor, you might increase the percentage estimate to 65 percent. If the company puts out a press release about pricing changes (but not a specific size or direction), that might only move the estimate to 67 percent. Wild swings in probability estimates are indications you had a fundamental misreading of the situation in the first place (or are now reading the tea leaves wrong).

- *Create supportive teams*: Teams of "regular" forecasters (not the best of the best) beat the aggregated forecasts of all the regular forecasters who worked individually. Teams of superforecasters were even better—and even better than prediction markets betting on the same question.[4] In fact, superforecasters became 50 percent more accurate in their individual predictions when they were put on teams with other superforecasters. Teams are better than individuals because they allow those teammates to share information and to stress test each other's ideas and estimates. As we'll see in chapter 7, building a team of competitive insight analysts that focus on different parts of the competitor's business—and who have regular discussions with each other—is the ideal organizational setup.

Superforecasters are comfortable with uncertainty—they don't need the world to be black and white. The predictions made at step 4 should adhere to this guidance and be assessed after the fact for whether they turned out to be right or wrong. The intent is not to punish those who were incorrect (or to unduly praise those who were correct) but to learn from the good and the bad in order to improve the organization's forecasting ability.[5] Hone this capability by continually updating your process for understanding the competitor to gain better insight into their mindset.

- Were there statements about their intentions that you missed? Add these to the list of sources you consult frequently to learn about what they are saying and planning to do. Are there foreign sources you forgot to include? Are there blog sites with industry insights that you hadn't been tracking? As you search for these additional sources, you will reduce the gaps in what you're hearing about the competitor.

- Did you misunderstand their capabilities or competencies? Or more accurately, did you misread what the competitor thinks their core competencies are? If you think they excel at execution, but they think they are good at marketing, you might see their move that has inefficient supply chain and production aspects as a bad decision. But if there is an uptick in the marketing spend, or in the number and types of distribution channels they use, you should look at their decision differently. It could be driven by an alternative functional expertise or by a set of resources you weren't aware of. Intangible assets, like relationships with platform partners, influencers, or government agencies, or knowledge of processes or content, are often the most difficult to see from outside the organization. After the fact, it can become easier to see how these intangibles were used, so build those updated insights into future analyses of the competitor.

- Did you focus on the wrong decision maker? Often times, very powerful CEOs may seem like they control all the decisions in their organization. But even the strongest CEO is tied up with investor relations and responding to emails and sitting in meetings, so others in the organization often will be making operational decisions. Think about who was ultimately responsible for the pricing or R&D or sourcing decisions: unless it's a major part of the competitor's business, those decisions will often be left to others to execute.

Figure out who it was most likely to be (often times, based on the person quoted or referenced in the press release, or the one who runs the division most prominently mentioned). Integrate the new information on the true decider into your process for understanding the competitor's decision-making.

Once you've refined your process for understanding the competitor, repeat steps 1 through 3 again to make another prediction. Assess the outcomes of this new prediction and then update your process from the postmortem analysis. Understanding competitors' mindsets is not about being right 100 percent of the time. It's about being right more often than you have been previously. Step 4 increases the reliability of your prediction process so that your overall average increases. As is true in any facet of life, the better your average success rate, the more successful you will be.

Leveraging Digital Technologies

The business world is awash in data, and "big data" strategies have revolutionized everything from supply chain management to customer insights. One area where it has not developed as strong a foundation is in business strategy, and two areas where it could potentially improve competitive strategy development are identifying early stage trends and anticipating complex market dynamics.[6]

Identifying early stage trends involve scanning for publicly available information of all sorts about a competitor to identify their organization-specific trends. For example, you should definitely use these tools to find correlations across data, such as the numerous patents competitors have been granted (e.g., which key scientific and strategic business words appear most often, how have they changed over time). However, artificial intelligence (AI) and machine learning (ML) have very limited ability to predict competitors, other than predicting them to continue on their current trajectory, precisely because of how AI and ML work. These technologies use past behavior to predict future outcomes and are calibrated to past trends because that's the existing data. They can show you when trends increase or decrease relative to historical rates, but they are not going to be able to identify how competitors will react to you—because you haven't made those strategic moves yet, so there is no data to calibrate against. And they can't identify true disruptions—which are significant deviations from historical trajectories.

Anticipating complex market dynamics involves creating intricate computational models. These also face challenges when predicting competitors because they can be highly sensitive to the model's underlying parameters and assumptions, especially if they are based on the actions and choices we would make or on the ones we would like the competitors to make. As we'll see in chapter 6, there are much better techniques for simulating competitors' behavior that incorporate the same data you would plug into the computational models but that allow more flexibility to adapt the simulation process as new decisions are made.[7]

AI and ML can help to collect and sort through data, and they can possibly uncover correlations across multiple different data points. Recall the discussion above about identifying the drivers, not the outcomes, of competitors' decisions: AI and ML tools can help you sort through all the voluminous information across publicly available sources to highlight when changes are occurring in those drivers. But they have yet to be able to do a good job of predicting discontinuities or responses to your strategic moves. Competitor data is historical and necessary for predicting the future, but it is not sufficient for generating insights. (Chapter 7 will have a discussion of competitive insight dashboards and the challenges involved with them.)

Asymmetry

Using the four-step process forces you to confront the asymmetry across different organizations. Not every competitor will communicate the same messages. Reading the announcements and press releases from senior leaders across multiple competitors can reveal whether they are all talking about the industry in the same way or if each one views the industry opportunities with varying levels of potential. This can not only give you insight into how the competitors collectively are approaching the market but also highlight the differences across the companies you compete with.

Similarly, each competitor will have a different set of assets, resources, capabilities, competencies, and starting points. This may seem obvious, but unless this is explicitly assessed, it's easy to fall into the mode of thinking that competitors are just like your company and therefore have the same opportunities you face. Just like each tailor has different combinations of needles and thread (and experience), each company in the industry has a different set of assets and resources to play with in developing and executing their strategies.

Finally, a CEO is not a CEO is not a CEO. In other words, each CEO is different along many dimensions: background, experiences, expertise, objectives, worldview, philanthropic interests, hobbies, and so forth. All of these come together to make each leader different. This applies not only to the CEO—it's also true for the rest of the C-suite and the division leadership as well as the competitor's collective leadership.

As far as agency problems, each organization is also different: centralized versus decentralized decision-making, compensation structures, decision-making speed, motivational drivers, and so on. It might be impossible to truly understand the full culture of your own organization, so I'm not suggesting that you have to perfectly understand how the competitor's organization lives and breathes. But you do need to start from an understanding that they do so differently, and to explicitly list all the ways their methods are different from yours. Otherwise, you will be no closer to understanding how their decision-making processes work or who truly owns the decision-making authority.

The Competition Is *Not* Irrational

One reason for the knee-jerk reaction to think of competitors as irrational is that it's very difficult to display true empathy for others. To really understand the mindset of our competitors, we need to walk the proverbial mile in their shoes. It isn't sufficient to merely think about what it would feel like to be in their shoes and walking; you have to actually slip on their dress shoes, feel the tightness of the leather, the lack of support in the soles, and the chafing of the heel. Only then can we really understand why they are walking on their hands—a seemingly irrational way to navigate a city street.

Empathy is the ability to understand what others are feeling and to share in their emotions. That definition has embedded in it a certain detachment. It's as if you're looking from the outside in at someone else who is struggling (or celebrating), understanding why they would be feeling the way they do and then deciding that you will feel that emotion too. But it's not as strong a feeling as actually experiencing that emotion yourself.

Being empathetic with your competition is incredibly challenging and not a natural way to think. After all, you're trying to take away market share from them. You're trying to prevent them from getting a foothold with your customers. You're trying to convince their best salespeople to come work for you. How can you be empathetic when you're trying to beat them?

For starters, being empathetic doesn't mean you have to be sympathetic. The difference between these two is often confused. Sympathy is feeling sorry for someone else's misfortune or supporting them in their (often negative) feelings. Empathy—understanding why they are sad about the situation, for example—doesn't mean you have to feel sorry for them. Sympathy means you feel sorry your competitor just got hit with a massive antitrust lawsuit. Empathy only means you understand how miserable it feels to be in their place. You don't have to be sympathetic toward them in that situation—you could even take it to an extreme and revel in their misfortune. But you'd better empathize with them and understand the stress the management is under, the fears they have of going to jail (or at minimum, losing their job), and the risk they may not feel like taking because of the regulatory scrutiny (or the increased risk they might take to divert attention and make others feel the same pressure).

Empathizing with your competitor in that situation will help you see that they might go on the attack with marketing messaging to prevent brand erosion. They might lower prices to stem the loss of market share, and they might try to poach some of your best managers to show that they're "cleaning house." If you didn't bother to empathize with them, what would you see? You'd see a company on the ropes with an antitrust investigation "lashing out" by advertising (with money they should be saving for any judgment or settlement), lowering prices (isn't that giving away money they'll need for the settlement?), and stealing talent from you. It would look like a vindictive attack against you and clearly an irrational reaction to the trouble they're in. But if you empathize and put yourself in their shoes, you'd realize that marketing and pricing will help the bottom line, which will help them weather the crisis. And the hiring away of your managers is necessary to increase the chances of a lower penalty. These aren't the actions of an irrational competitor lashing out but a perfectly rational response to prevent a total collapse of the business (and their careers).

Being empathetic forces you to ask a key question: "If I were she, what would I do?" True empathy requires that you imagine you are actually in her shoes—feeling everything she's feeling professionally and personally. The crux of the problem is that as humans, we're pretty bad at *cognitive* empathy, which focuses on our ability to understand another's perspective (as opposed to *emotional* empathy, which focuses on our concern for the emotions of others).[8] Recent neuroscientific research has explored whether there is a biological basis for empathy, and most of this research focuses on emotional empathy. Scientists have found evidence for "mirror neurons" in the brain—specific neurons that fire when an individual is observing someone else performing a task or displaying a certain emotion.[9] For example, when we see someone else pick up a tea cup, the neurons in our brain that control the movement of our hand and fingers for grasping activate. Or if we see someone smile, the neurons that activate the facial muscles involved in smiling fire. Even if we don't move our hand and fingers, or smile, our brain acts like we do. This mirroring effect is a form of empathy: we experience others' actions and emotions as if they were our own.

As business leaders, trying to work our way up by showing that we can beat all comers, it's even harder to shift gears and view the world from the competitor's point of view. In particular, recent research has shown that mirror neurons fired less often in subjects who had greater social power status.[10] The implication is that these naturally occurring systems that help us empathize with others are less responsive as we gain more power—which is exactly what happens as business leaders move up the corporate hierarchy. Senior leaders—the ones tasked with crafting competitive strategies—are those least likely to be able to empathize innately with the competitors' viewpoint. These leaders must actively work to put themselves in the mindset of their competitors.

The competition is not irrational—they merely need to be understood. Applying the four-step framework can provide you with the deliberate nudge to think about the competition as well as a structured way of analyzing them objectively.

What sets this framework apart from most other competitive strategy ideas is that it helps explain "why" the competitor made a particular move rather than detailing "what happened." It's necessary to track what happened in the market along many dimensions (e.g., their market share went up, a competitor's net promoter score went up), but if you don't understand why it happened (e.g., they lowered their prices versus they introduced a new product, they spent more on marketing versus they improved their customer service), you won't be well positioned to counter their moves.

The same is true for the best coaches. They don't just check the wins-and-losses columns in the sports section. They focus on understanding why the competition improved from last year or is on a winning streak during the season. They keep their jobs because they are experts at staying one step ahead of the competition. They listen to what the opponents say, dissect film of what they do in games, are always observant of players added to (or cut from) others' rosters, and explore the background and history of the opposing coaches. You don't have to be a sports fan to master these same techniques. Apply them to your current challenges to get inside the mindset of the competitor and create your own advantage.

2   Thinking about All Kinds of Competitors

Mixed martial arts (MMA) has been one of the fastest growing sports in the past few decades. It grew out of a debate between enthusiasts of different fighting styles: which combat techniques were the "best"? The original organizers decided to pit wrestlers against boxers, jiu-jitsu specialists opposite taekwondo experts, and Muay Thai fighters in the octagon ring with kickboxers. They paired these specialties against each other in every possible combination.

These fighters employ coaches and trainers to help them, but unlike the analogy used in chapter 1, these coaches have had to look outside their specialty to understand how to defend against threats and attacks that were out of the ordinary muscle memory ingrained in their fighters. The coaches themselves have had to learn new techniques and train their fighters to combine multiple styles into their repertoire, and they've created coaching teams composed of experts in various techniques to provide the best guidance. What has developed over time is a new mix of fighting techniques that are constantly adjusting to meet the skills of the next opponent in the ring.

The four steps highlighted in the previous chapter can be used to gain a better understanding of any competitor. This chapter focuses primarily on how to understand competitors that don't appear to fit the typical mold and therefore seem especially difficult to diagnose. The previous chapter made an implicit assumption that you were analyzing an existing competitor within a market you both were contesting. However, we can also apply the framework to entrants who might leverage

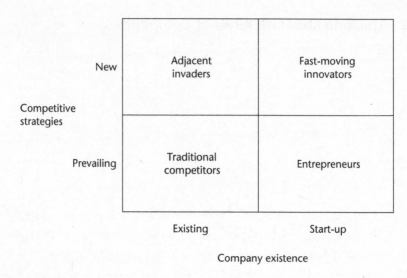

Figure 2.1
Categorizing different competitor types

current strategic techniques, invaders from adjacent industries, and disruptive innovators. More generally, we can categorize competitors by comparing two dimensions:

1. Are they employing competitive strategies currently prevailing in your industry?
2. Are they an existing company?

The 2 × 2 matrix in figure 2.1 shows which types of companies fall into each of the four boxes.

This book focuses primarily on the lower left quadrant—the current set of known competitors—as this is the group you are most likely to need to understand. However, all of the frameworks can be applied to the other three quadrants as you become more sophisticated in building out competitive insights. This chapter will focus on those other three boxes.

Adjacent Invaders

The chapter 1 framework forces you to think about the competitor's holistic organization. As we discussed at the end of the previous chapter, companies have different starting positions and operate in a different mix of sectors, so they should make different choices. For example, Netflix is primarily a content delivery company that shifted into producing their own content for streaming. Hulu is a joint venture of several production companies (initially NBC and Fox and then adding Disney, and then becoming majority Disney owned after the latter's acquisition of Fox). Disney+ is a proprietary streaming service based on a deep library of a century's worth of content. Apple has entered the streaming sector to help with the sale of devices (and to diversify their revenue stream). And Google has focused YouTube on smaller-scale production by individuals (not large production houses), though they also offer live TV streaming of a subset of channels—over the air and cable (as does Hulu). Each one of these players is playing in the streaming space with a different set of assets and resources at their disposal, and so they are making different choices in how they compete in the streaming space.

In the early 2010s, I was involved in a strategic discussion with a television services provider about the future of the industry precipitated by the rise of streaming services and over-the-top content provision. We created a war gaming lite exercise (see chapter 6) to help them understand how other competitors in the market might invest in the coming years. At that time, Disney had a small ownership stake in Hulu, and Netflix was about five years into their streaming journey. The one consistent concern that kept coming out of the discussions was not any of the potential extension moves by existing players but a large foray into the streaming space by Disney. This foreshadowed Disney+ by about five years and was driven by the constant refrain of "But they have so much fantastic content, they can't afford *not* to get into the space. If they do, they'll almost certainly win." The other key insight that emerged was "Whoever wins will be the company that helps the viewer find relevant content easier," which we've seen has been a key resource leveraged by Amazon and Apple through the use of their Alexa and Siri assistants to help viewers find shows on their streaming platforms.

Corporate scope refers to all the things an organization as a whole does to enhance or support what they could do in any one particular business unit. Google not only owns YouTube but also Android, Google Maps, and other business divisions, and almost all of them are centrally focused around searching the internet and connecting users with information. Companies that compete with Google in one of those spaces must pay attention to changes they make with any other division to assess the potential impact on their business.

Procter and Gamble (P&G) has in recent years shed businesses to get down to baby, feminine, and family care; beauty; health care; grooming; and fabric and home care business units in their portfolio.[1] P&G's website states that their "integrated growth strategy . . . position[s] P&G well to continue to serve the heightened needs and new behaviors of consumers and our retail and distributor partners."[2] If you are a shampoo manufacturer that competes with P&G in the beauty space, you also need to deliberate over how P&G will use their consumer understanding and the habits and lifestyles of those purchasing their products to enhance their shampoo lines. Will they develop more "mobile" shampoos that can be applied outside the home? Will they create shampoos with different scents that activate in different conditions? Will they invent a product that uses less water for rinsing to address climate-related consumer choices? And how will the understanding they develop of their retail and distributor partners with regard to the other products P&G supplies help them better position their shampoo products? P&G will also engage in chemical R&D to improve the product attributes, to be sure, but the overall corporate focus on consumer behaviors and distributors/retailers will also inform their choices in the shampoo segment.

Another common source of adjacent invaders comes from others in the value chain that disintermediate your company. The classic example of this is when Levi's started selling jeans and clothing directly to consumers through their own retail outlets, thereby cutting out the department store distribution channel that had been a large contributor of sales previously. The shift to online sales from many consumer goods companies has amplified this trend, and it's also occurring with business-to-business industries. I helped a chemicals company think about how to manage the pivot from selling through distributors to selling directly to customers through a proprietary online portal. The upheaval to the existing distributors was going to create challenges with ensuring consistent delivery to end users, but it was necessary in the long run.

By paying attention to corporate scope, you are less likely to be blindsided by a competitor that leverages their corporate competencies in support of the individual division against which you compete. Think about your own organization: don't you use the best of the rest of the organization to succeed? Perhaps not always, but you must at least some of the time. Then why assume that your competitor is so strictly siloed that they won't leverage corporate resources? Unless your previous analysis revealed that they are hyperdecentralized and use no shared corporate services, you should assume they do. And frankly, it's rare that any organization has no cross-corporate coordination, so you better have a good reason to assume that's the case.

Corporate scope insights also help identify invaders from adjacent industries. Companies that move into new industries almost always leverage core capabilities and competencies that help them succeed in their current markets. They search for other sectors where those same competencies and capabilities are also drivers of success. If you want to seek out who might move into your territory in the coming years, you should focus on the key capabilities that drive success in your industry. Seek out those who already possess and excel at those skills as they are most likely to be potential future threats.

Entrepreneurs

Entrepreneurs primarily reside in the lower right quadrant of figure 2.1. They present an interesting challenge with competitive insight on two fronts:

1. How should you track competitors if you're an entrepreneur and new to the industry?

2. How should incumbents go about getting inside the head of an entrepreneur?

The challenge an entrepreneur faces in understanding their competitors mostly comes from the lack of a critical resource: time. Entrepreneurs have so many spinning plates to keep in the air that it's hard for them to find time to go through the four-step process outlined in chapter 1. However, that doesn't mean they can't use the same methodology to analyze the competitive landscape. In the next chapter, we'll explore one particular question that is extraordinarily important for entrepreneurs: how will incumbents react to our entry into the market or the introduction of our new product? Entrepreneurs have to both master the internally focused job of developing the right product or service and the processes and organization to be able to deliver it to the market, and have a sense of where, when, and how incumbents will react to their market entry or growth.

Since entrepreneurs don't have a large organizational bench among whom they can assign the competitive insight research, they should start in a much more targeted way than a larger incumbent would. An entrepreneur should start with the one or two competitors they will be directly trying to go after with their new product or service. As they were developing the idea, they were probably thinking at some point, "We can do it better than Company X can." The entrepreneur should home in on understanding that "Company X" (or X and Y). Begin with the step 1 questions: What are they saying about the subsector you are entering? Have they mentioned any new entrants or entry threats to the market? How have they reacted in the past to newer entrants?

In step 2, the entrepreneur should focus on the individual division or region they will be competing against—contrary to what was said above, they should not worry as much about the corporate scope at this point. The larger incumbents will probably start combating the entrant with a more targeted approach rather than using every resource available in the corporation. In particular, the entrepreneur should ask "What are the resources that their size affords them the ability to use that we can't use because we're new and small?" Larger incumbents will likely start with these large-player resources. Finally, the entrepreneur should focus on the division-level manager who will be tasked with competing against them (step 3 of the framework). It's not always obvious who this will be, but as the entrepreneur has started to explore the industry to see how they could fit in, they have probably developed some insight on who are the key individuals. These are the ones to focus on.

The entrepreneur should then make a prediction but this time they should be much more vigilant about tracking the competitive response. Entrepreneurs often don't have the luxury of failing multiple times before ultimately finding success (at least, with the same start-up). In step 4, entrepreneurs should track and adjust as quickly as possible to find gaps in the incumbents' competitive response in which to survive, thrive, and grow.

These tips for entrepreneurs do not guarantee success, of course. They could mistakenly listen to the wrong competitors, misunderstand the extent that incumbents will bring other resources to bear, or not identify the true decision maker. But these tips will increase the chances that the new venture can survive the incumbents' competitive responses. If you were the entrepreneur, would you rather ignore the competitors and hope that your new venture will survive the marketplace, or would you try to get at least some understanding of where those competitive pressures might come from, better positioning you to hold them off?

The flip side is developing competitive insight on entrepreneurs from the incumbent's point of view. How can these four steps be applied to a new entrant into the industry when there is no existing data to rely on? Let's walk through the process to see how it still applies. First, what has the entrepreneur said publicly about the market or their company? Are there any documents they shared with angel or venture capital investors (if they are not protected by nondisclosure agreements)? Many times, new ventures will have websites or Facebook pages that are up and running before they launch—or in early stages of the launch—to drum up support or business (sometimes including simplified versions of their pitch decks). Read what the entrepreneurs are saying on their websites about their product or service, launch plans, and target markets.

Second, look at the resources their company has to use. Again, many new companies will announce they have secured venture funding or competition grants. If you search the internet using the new company's name, you can find information about who has joined the venture and who is backing them.

Third, and possibly more important, research the founders' backgrounds. Look at their LinkedIn profile to see what previous entrepreneurial efforts they might have launched. Were they successful? How many previous attempts did they make? Are they serial entrepreneurs or first-time founders? If serial entrepreneurs, try to find information on their prior companies. Were they successful, and did the founders cash out to move on? Or were they not successful? Were they in your same industry (in which case you can do more digging to find out why they failed or moved on)? Or if they were in another industry where you have contacts, call those resources up to try and find out about the founders. Serial entrepreneurs are typically more successful because they can build upon their past experiences of having started a company. It also means they are highly likely to leverage their past experience, so understanding what they did before will help you predict what they're likely to do this time. If the founders of the venture you're investigating have no prior experience, that's important information to know too.

The founders' LinkedIn profiles will also provide valuable information about their prior corporate work experience. Learn about their functional background. As with new CEOs of large corporations, founders who worked in marketing will likely try to leverage that knowledge in their entrepreneurial venture. Have the founders worked at larger companies, and is the venture in the same industry? What do you know about how that larger company works? Compare that to the new venture. Do you think it will operate similarly to how the large company works (i.e., an ex-employee saw an opportunity the big company could have undertaken but wanted to do it themselves)? Or does the new venture require a completely different operating model (i.e., the ex-employee was frustrated by the inability to execute their plan within the larger company, so they struck out on their own with a new process)? In either case, you can now develop an understanding of the entrepreneur's mindset.

In general, use the founders' history to gain insight into how they think and approach business. Current plans or statements on their new organization's website, information from past jobs on their LinkedIn profile, "likes" of other businesses or their prior ventures that might still have Facebook pages—these are all sources to develop insight into the mind of the entrepreneur. And if you're really lucky, you might be able to use your own network to find someone to talk with about the founders.

None of these efforts will guarantee absolutely perfect insight into the mind of the entrepreneur. As with all competitive insight, it's about increasing the chances that you will make accurate predictions about your competitor. It's possible there will be an entrepreneur who will come out of nowhere or about whom there isn't any useful information. The good news is that it's rare for these types of entrepreneurs to crash upon the scene and make a large incumbent suffer huge financial losses within days or months. There is time to learn and improve your understanding of what the entrepreneur is doing, but that will only happen if you take the time to look outward and observe who those potential competitors might be. Ignoring them and only looking inward will guarantee you are surprised time and time again.

Fast-Moving Innovators

What should a competitive insight analyst do in a fast-moving industry, where the pace of change means the competitive strategist can't solely rely on historical information? These types of industries are where we often face the kinds of disruptive innovation found in the upper right quadrant of figure 2.1. The competitors in this quadrant could be entrepreneurs, existing players from your industry coming from other geographies, or incumbents currently focused on other customer segments.

In these types of markets, like some high-tech sectors or apparel, the four-step process does not change. You still need to listen to the competition, understand the toys they have to play with, determine who's making the decision, make a prediction, and then update the process as necessary. The difference is that you obviously have less time to do any of the four steps, so focus on the decisions that matter most. Where has the competition surprised you? The types of new products they introduced? The technology embedded in them? The price at which they sold their products? The customer groups they targeted? Narrow your focus to applying the four steps to those specific decisions.

Let's look at new product introduction, a common competitive challenge in fast-moving industries. What statements has the company made about their product development process? What articles have been written about it? What are the assets, resources, and capabilities that allow them to introduce products quicker than you? Who's in charge of that portion of their business? What has that individual said about the process? What was the previous stop for that leader, and how long have they been in their current role? These kinds of questions will provide an overview of the competitor, but then look deeper into step 2: examine the assets and resources and processes they use. Is it a nimble supply chain, flexible supply agreements with vendors, consumer-focused big data analysis to track trends, or some combination of these?

If they are a tech company launching a new software product, how long does it take for each version? How many small bets are they making at any one time that will generate the churn of rapid hits? Understand whether the development time for each individual product or service is short (in which case you need to increase the speed at which you make predictions and track changes), or if the competitor is very good at managing a portfolio of opportunities (which means you need to do a better job of coordinating across competitive insight analysts and data in your organization).

If they are an apparel company, what type of consumer information are they tracking? Are they also making portfolio plays of bringing lots of products to market and then ramping up the delivery and sales of those that sell well? Or are they observant of consumer trends and launch when the time is right? The way in which they are able to beat you to the market will provide insight into why they are successful.

This sounds reasonable, but could this have helped actual companies? What about Marriott and the Airbnb disruption? How could any incumbent have foreseen this? They easily could have. Airbnb launched in 2008, but VRBO was founded in 1995, a full thirteen years before. (As a personal note, I used VRBO in 2009, which seemed like a "new" service to me. I had not yet heard of Airbnb. It can take time for new products to break through and become mainstream.) Not only was VRBO a precursor, but they were acquired by HomeAway in 2006, which was one year after the latter was formed. There was action in the "individual unit rental by owner" market even though neither had the exact same business model as Airbnb. There was enough activity that it easily could have been on Marriott's radar.

In another classic example, Red Bull was launched in 1987 in Europe, although the company was founded in 1984. Red Bull was based on a drink developed in Thailand in 1976 but didn't enter the US market until 1996. Could Coca-Cola and Pepsi have foreseen this? Of course! If they had been monitoring local drinks in developing markets, they would have known of this new offering.[3]

The point of both of these examples is not to say that Marriott, Coca-Cola, or Pepsi should have mimicked the new entrants. It only demonstrates they should have known about these potential entrants. And in fact, it did *not* make sense for Marriott to have invested in building a room-sharing app before Airbnb. The owners of the hotels that license the Marriott brand names under the management agreements would not have been pleased to know that Marriott would be planning to disintermediate them. If the hotel owners could not have immediately canceled their contracts to find another hotel management partner, they almost certainly would have left when the contract was up for renewal. Similarly, Coca-Cola and Pepsi would have been placing their strong brand valuation on the line to produce an energy drink in the early 1990s.

Just because you're aware of the entrepreneur doesn't mean you should attack them, or can attack them, head-to-head. Marriott should *not* have redesigned their whole business model to block Airbnb nor should Coca-Cola or Pepsi to counter Red Bull. Just because we see a new start-up succeeding or disrupting a market doesn't mean the incumbents were fooled. It does mean, however, that the incumbents need to constantly be scanning to identify those disrupters and make plans to mitigate their impact to the greatest extent possible.

Sometimes what seems to be a fast-moving competitor is really a fast-moving set of competitors that are leap-frogging each other. This makes the challenge of understanding any one competitor more difficult, but again, simplify the process by focusing on the primary competitive challenges you face: pricing, new products or services, technological developments, and so on. Look at those choices across a subset of competitors and use that broader understanding to deduce trends.

Public versus Private Competitors

Finally, there is one governance structure spanning all four quadrants that is important to call out: are there differences in applying the chapter 1 framework to private versus publicly traded companies? We can find privately held competitors in each of the four boxes of figure 2.1, and the same four steps will apply. In the case of entrepreneurs' companies (which are almost always privately held), we've seen there isn't much difference. It's a bit harder to obtain the necessary information to complete the four-step process, but that's about it. This is true more generally with larger private companies. It's harder to obtain the needed information about them, but remember, even publicly traded companies don't have to reveal everything about themselves in their regulatory filings.

Private companies can still provide press releases, they will still attend industry conferences, there will still be journal articles written about them, and their leaders will still make the occasional public speech. Determining the assets, resources, and capabilities of private companies requires the same type of detective work as for public companies. Even though the latter might have to disclose some information about their number of employees and plant locations in regulatory filings, they don't have to list new equipment, details on contracts with partners, descriptions of patent filings, brand strength and reputation, or organizational processes. You'll still have to put these data together from secondary sources like news articles, press releases, announcements from vendors, patent applications, announcements from partners, and many of the other types of sources you would use for uncovering information about public competitors. Similarly, gathering information on private companies' leaders uses the same information sources we've discussed for the public companies.

Take Cargill, for example. In 2021 they were the largest privately held company in the United States, according to Forbes.[4] Their website looks similar to that of any other large, publicly held company: business segments, information about the company (including information on the executive team), a list of products and services, and a news center with press releases, speeches, and presentations. Cargill even provides an annual report. It isn't as detailed as required for a public filing but provides business segment information, high-level revenue results, and commentary from the CEO on their performance.

Of course, not all private companies are this transparent. But the rest of the Forbes private top 10—Koch Industries, Publix Super Markets, Mars, H-E-B, Reyes Holdings, Pilot Company, C&S Wholesale Grocers, Enterprise Holdings, and Fidelity Investments—had information about their businesses and press releases on their main website or specific sites set up to handle this information, while Koch, Mars, Pilot, C&S, and Enterprise also had leadership biographies posted. So while it may seem impossible to understand a privately held company, it's not. You won't have full insight into them, but then again, that's not possible with publicly traded companies either. The point is to gather more information than you previously had so you'll have a better picture about them than you would with no investigation.

That said, there are two particular ownership structures to highlight with regard to understanding privately held competitors: private equity

owned and family owned. When examining private equity–owned competitors, you should focus on the investment firm's portfolio and look
at the history of how they've managed the firms they acquired. They
usually bring in new leadership to the acquisition, so from where do
they find those new leaders? Do they manage the company for growth
or for a quick sale? How long have they typically held companies before
selling them off? Do they seem to use a particular playbook for how to
turn around a struggling acquisition?

For family-owned private companies, it's important to develop an
understanding of the broader family relations and power structure. Just
because a daughter is nominally in charge of the organization doesn't
mean the parents aren't still making many of the larger strategic decisions. Articles written about the family dynamics of large, privately
held organizations are a great resource for developing a picture of how
these relationships influence the company's decision-making.

Whether the competitor has a different governance structure, comes
from a different industry, employs new strategic techniques, or is constantly innovating to disrupt the established dynamics, you can still
gain insight into why they behave the way they do by applying the
lessons from chapter 1 with slight modifications. An MMA fighter still
needs to build muscle and develop stamina and endurance through car-
dio training—those basics still apply. But by understanding how their
next opponent is different, and by honing their techniques to counter those specific asymmetries, aspiring combatants can increase the
chance they will ultimately wind up holding the championship belt.

3   How Will They React?

It is said that chess grand masters can analyze between ten and fifteen moves ahead in a game. They can only do this by incorporating their opponent's moves too. They work through the possible choices they can make and the potential moves the opponent could make and then assess which of their options gives them the best chance of gaining an advantage. A chess grand master knows there are sequences of moves that an opponent would take—and that she would take in response—having memorized many possible ways in which the game could play out over the course of a dozen moves.

If you've ever had the misfortune to play chess against someone who is really good (not necessarily a grand master, even), then you likely found it very frustrating because they seemed to block every move you made. You led with a bishop only to find that your opponent captured your knight while simultaneously blocking your bishop. Or you maneuvered your rook into the middle of the board by castling with the king to set up an attack, only to find that you were on your heels defending the king as he was trapped in the corner.

That's what it feels like sometimes when we contemplate our strategic business moves: no matter what brilliant idea we come up with, by the time we actually execute and bring it to market, the competition has already beaten us to the punch. Or they will be ready to pounce from the back row with their queen and throttle our strategy to check and possibly mate us. So how do we overcome these fears and arrive at a better understanding of what our competitors are capable of doing and what they are contemplating doing? We'll start by thinking through how they might respond to our strategic choices and then move on to assessing what their proactive moves might be in the next chapter.

In 1979, Anheuser-Busch, the largest beer company in the United States, decided to start manufacturing and selling a line of snack foods to complement their beer sales. When people become thirsty from eating salty snacks, the thinking went, they will need something to satiate their thirst. What better to reach for than for a nice, cold Budweiser? The company's Eagle Snacks brand soon took off—literally—as Anheuser-Busch began by marketing the chips and pretzels to airlines and also selling them to taverns. Both channels served Anheuser-Busch's core strategic rationale: a captive audience who would be thirsty and become even thirstier as they consumed more salty snack foods. The Eagle Snacks products were very popular and had soon established a following among the jet set and the pub crawlers.

At this point, Anheuser-Busch had a choice to make. They could either continue to sell this complementary product and reap higher profit margins since there would be little need for additional marketing expense, or they could expand the channel footprint into the grocery, convenience, and liquor store markets, where packaged beer was purchased. Again, the strategic and marketing rationale made sense. You're in the liquor store and grab some beer, and then on your way to pay, you spot some Eagle Snacks pretzels and think, "Mmm, those would go great with this beer."

Anheuser-Busch ultimately decided to expand in the early 1980s, right into the territory that Frito-Lay controlled and dominated. Up until that point, Frito-Lay was probably not happy about the sales that Anheuser-Busch was making to airlines and taverns. But it was a niche segment of the market and not where Frito-Lay generated their largest sales volume. The packaged food store channels—grocery, convenience, and liquor stores—were, however, and Frito-Lay was not about to let Anheuser-Busch encroach on that turf without a fight.

And fight they did. Frito-Lay instituted across-the-board price cuts. They added extra drivers and restocking salespeople to visit their retail channel outlets to ensure there was a steady supply of Lays potato chips and Rold Gold pretzels clogging the shelves and ringing up the registers. And to ensure that the consumer's hand reached for a Frito-Lay product, they tripled the amount of money spent on advertising.

Anheuser-Busch's Eagle Snacks lasted for seventeen years, at which point they decided to shut the division. They found no buyer for Eagle Snacks, so they sold the trademark for $10–$20 million to P&G (who never used it for their own branded products). Anheuser-Busch sold four of their five manufacturing plants for $135 million . . . to Frito-Lay. Anheuser-Busch took a write-off of $206 million on the rest of the business.

The story is not intended to highlight that companies make bad decisions. As the story points out, there was a clear strategic and organizational rationale to this product line: the products were complementary, they started small in a niche market, and they expanded when they had figured out their products and processes. What this story does make clear, though, is that you must pay attention to the reactions of competitors. Just because you are successful in one niche market doesn't mean you can expand to broader markets. Success in one region doesn't imply global dominance. And focusing too much on your own products and processes, and your current customers, can blind you to the potential brick wall that competitors can erect in your path when they feel threatened enough by your future growth plans.

The whole point of understanding your competitors is to be better able to predict what moves they may make in the future. Sure, it might make for interesting cocktail party fodder at industry association conventions to wow your fellow industry participants with insights into others at the meetings. But it really only does you good if you can take those predictions and use them to better craft your own strategy. This could take the shape of positioning your moves so they can't be countered easily by your competitors, taking positions in submarkets you know they won't contest, or crafting your public communications to throw them off the scent.

This chapter and the next will build upon the four-step process we outlined in the previous chapters by exploring two particularly challenging competitor moves most companies face:

1. How will competitors react to the strategic move we are contemplating?
2. Will the competitor make a new strategic move of their own, and what might that be?

To address these, we will refine step 4 from chapter 1: how can you predict the competitor's behavior? This chapter will tackle the first question,[1] and I'll address the second in the next chapter.

How Will My Competitors Respond to My Latest Brilliant Strategy?

When businesspeople develop new strategies, a great deal of work goes into the effort: testing, meeting, refining, meeting again, assessing, meeting once more, even more meetings, more assessment, and then finally reaching a decision. Unfortunately, one element that is often ignored in this process is thinking about how competitors will react to the new strategy and what that implies for its potential success. Support for this goes beyond anecdotal stories.

In 2005, David Montgomery, Marian Chapman Moore, and Joel Urbany tested what businesspeople did when they thought about making strategic decisions.[2] They interviewed business executives about the key considerations they used in a strategic decision made in the past year and then used the answers to assess whether the executives had used certain analyses to help make their decisions. A little over half of the executives were asked about a retrospective pricing decision, while the others were asked about a past decision to introduce a new product. Internal factors, like capabilities and assets and resources at the executive's company, were used over 80 percent of the time for both kinds of decisions. Customer information was used for 75 percent of the new product introductions but just over 50 percent of the pricing decisions. Overall market conditions were factored in 60 percent of the time for new products (only 44 percent of the time for pricing).

So far, these results are as expected. (Though some of you might wonder what the other 20 percent were thinking by ignoring the internal factors.) When it came to competitors, it appears the executives were aware of who they would be facing. Over two-thirds of the time, competitors were at least mentioned by the interviewee, and almost 60 percent of the time the executive talked about past or current competitive behavior. But the research gets interesting when the interviewees were assessed as having debated the expected *future* competitor behavior or expected *future* competitor response. These last two involve predicting what competitors will do. Here, the executives were largely silent. For pricing decisions, only 11 percent considered future competitor behavior, and only 5 percent talked about future competitor reactions! The percentages for new product introductions were even worse: 7 percent discussed future competitor behavior, and only 2 percent considered future competitor responses. Less than 10 percent of the time these executives recalled thinking about how their competitors were going to react to the new strategic initiative they were going to launch!

The researchers determined whether they might just have gotten a few anomalous strategic decisions by asking the interviewees, "What questions would you ask yourself if you were making the same decision again?" Surely, the executives would realize they had neglected the competitive response. At least some of them must have come up against strong reactions in the market, which in hindsight would have led them to consider integrating competitor responses in future decisions. Unfortunately, not enough did. The internal, customer, market, competitor, and past competitor behavior factors were all about the same as before. Eleven percent of the pricing decision executives said they would assess future competitor behavior, and 18 percent would forecast expected future pricing reactions. Only 2 percent of the new product executives expected to think about future competitor behavior, while 5 percent would discuss future competitor responses.

Fewer than one in five executives did not think that assessing potential future competitive reactions to their proposed pricing strategy was
relevant. Pricing is essentially the easiest of all strategic levers to pull,
and these executives didn't think it would matter how hard competitors might pull their pricing lever in response.

Why do companies ignore the competitive response? As we've discussed, it's primarily because competitors are thought to be irrational.
And who can understand, much less predict, what an irrational person
will do in the future? But since competitors are not irrational, we can
better predict their potential reactions—we just need a structured way
to analyze the problem.

When thinking about how a competitor will react to your planned
strategic initiative, ask yourself three key questions:

1. Will it matter to them?
2. What will they consider?
3. What will they choose to do?

We will work through these questions in order.

Will It Matter to Them?

Every business person has to deal with dozens of planned and unplanned
issues every day (possibly, more of the latter than the former). They have
to put out fires from customers and suppliers, respond to impromptu
meetings from superiors, and work on developing their own new strategies. Think about the time you spend each day: how much "free" time
do you have to sit back and scan the industry landscape? How much
time is spent responding to emails (or starting your own email chain)?
How much time is tied up sitting in meetings, or preparing for meetings, or sending out "next steps" messages after meetings?

In that context, the first question to ask is, "Will this strategic initiative really matter to them?" On the surface, the obvious answer is
"yes." This is a strategic move you've spent months planning, designing, building, testing, and refining. It has taken up a lot of your time

and effort, so of course this will matter to your competitors. But this is really the self-focused trap we've been talking about: you're looking at the world from your perspective, not from the viewpoint of the competitor. You need to assess this strategic change with your empathetic glasses: how will the competitors view this new strategy? To answer that, there are three subquestions you must address.

Will They See the Threat?

The most obvious subquestion is whether the competitor will even notice that you're making this strategic change. The general inclination is to assume yes: every competitor is out there just trying to think of ways to beat you or to pounce on your idea and kill it. But in order for the competition to react to you that quickly, they have to be aware of the strategic change you're implementing.

There are two primary reasons why the competition might not observe your new move. The first is that you are making it in an area of the market in which the competitor isn't focused. For example, you might be conducting a test market in a geographic region where they have a small presence, or you might be selling through a distribution channel they are not currently using. In China, most companies collect market data on tier 1 cities and some tier 2 cities. If you were to launch in tier 3 cities, it could likely fly under the radar of your competitor.

These blind spots might also arise because of the decentralized nature of the competitor's organization. One large multinational building materials company was facing this issue. They were set up on a regional basis, with each manager having full profit and loss (P&L) responsibility for their country. This made sense operationally since building materials can be very difficult to ship long distances and construction practices and demand factors can vary greatly once you cross a national border. The challenge was that their primary competitor was also operating in dozens of the same countries, and the corporate leaders could see how the competitor's pricing and product introduction patterns were similar across geographies. If they lowered prices in one country, they would often lower them in other similar countries in the next few months. Since the company was set up in a decentralized manner, the regional managers were blinded to these trends in the other countries.

The second reason the competitor might not see your strategic move is if they are really distracted by other efforts at their company. They might not be able to look outside their organization and see what's going on with their competitors. The fires raging within the competitor's organization could be so intense that they are focusing all of their energy on trying to put them out. Or the competitor might be so deep in the midst of completing the implementation of their own new strategic move that they aren't focused on how others are acting in the market.

There is a classic psychological research study demonstrating this effect, referred to as inattentional blindness. In the study, participants were asked to watch a video of people in black or white shirts passing basketballs between themselves. The participants were asked to count specific occurrences, like passes between different colored shirts, or types of passes, or the total number of passes of all the balls. In the middle of the video, a person wearing a gorilla suit walked in the middle of the basketball players, thumped its chest, and then proceeded off screen. At the end of the video, the research participants were asked if anything unusual had happened. On average, half of subjects reported they didn't notice the gorilla at all.[3] In follow-up studies, when subjects were asked to intentionally look for the gorilla, some still didn't notice it. Even those who did see the gorilla missed other changes the researchers made to the video. Focus too much on one important task and you have a hard time observing changes around you.

This applies to organizations too. Think of your own daily routine. You might read the news when you arrive at the office or over lunch. You might catch up on the latest reports from the industry association or other aggregators. But on those days when there is one problem after another, and just as one fire gets put out, another two sprout up, do you still take the time to read the news? Or catch up on those reports? We all triage and make sure immediate needs are taken care of first. The same happens with your competitors: if they are distracted by big changes in their organization, it will be hard for them to take time to look outward for signs of change.

Will They Feel the Threat?

But let's assume the competitor does know that you are planning this new strategic shift and they are aware it's coming. The second sub-question is whether they will even feel the impact. For major strategic changes, this is probably the case, at least from your perspective. If you weren't planning to have a big impact with your strategic shift, you probably wouldn't be considering it. Once again, we have to ask, from the competitor's vantage point, if they will feel the threat.

One way to consider this is from the asymmetric perspective we discussed in chapter 1. Not every company has the same market share positions, geographic coverage, or product portfolio. Unless you're launching a full line of SKUs (stock-keeping units) to take on every single possible offering in the market, you will have different impacts on different competitors. Take Coca-Cola and Pepsi. In some countries, Coke has the stronger brand, and in others it's Pepsi. If Coke were to introduce a new product in countries where they have the leading market share, there would be less impact on Pepsi's performance than in a country where Pepsi has the leading position. And if Coca-Cola were to introduce a new sports drink, where Pepsi's Gatorade has such a strong positioning, they would likely garner a stronger reaction than if they introduced a new energy drink or bottled tea. That's not to imply that Pepsi doesn't care about these other products or the potential lost sales in the markets where they are already trailing, but it's a matter of priorities. If your strategic move won't have a material impact on your competitor, they may not respond (at least not significantly).

This ties in with the second factor that affects whether the competitor will feel the threat: the decision maker. Every senior manager has a set of explicit—or implicit—targets they must reach each time period. Part of their decision on whether the geography or product portfolio will be impacted by your move is based on being able to hit their targets. Granted, you cannot call them and ask what their performance contract clauses and thresholds are. But observing them will help you understand what metrics they focus on: Do they talk about market share or earnings? What are the senior executive performance bonus structures as listed in the proxy statements (and therefore which metrics matter for the corporation overall)? Do their past decisions seem to indicate a focus on market share or profitability or top-line growth?

If those managers have already exceeded their threshold targets, will they risk that superior performance by engaging in a slash-and-burn response that you feel your strategic move would deserve? Think back to the Anheuser-Busch example at the beginning of this chapter. Frito-Lay did not aggressively respond to Eagle Snacks while they were sold in airline and tavern distribution channels. Sure, it took away some potential sales, but it would have risked the bigger portion of their business to respond in a serious manner. Once Anheuser-Busch took that step into Frito-Lay's largest market share channels, they had no choice but to defend their turf. At that point, they would have felt the threat if Eagle Snacks had been as successful there as they had been to date in the airline and tavern channels.

Will They Prioritize the Threat?

The third influence on whether your strategic move will matter to your competitors is whether responding will take precedence over everything else their organization needs to accomplish. This is slightly different from the first subquestion of their recognizing the threat. Here, we're assuming they see the threat and they recognize they'll be impacted by your move. However, their internal triage process indicates that, in the grand scheme of things, reacting does not matter.

One prime example is if the competitor has recently undertaken a large strategic effort of their own. If they have, reversing course can be a huge challenge. The internal buy-in, and investor acceptance, is at risk if the competitor changes direction. Rapid shifts in strategic direction, without a clear understanding by internal and external stakeholders, can lead to organizational paralysis. Another example is if the competitor has recently completed—or is near completing—a large acquisition.

The process of integrating two companies can consume both organizations, and in the long term, the competitor might think that successful integration is more important than responding to your initiative. On the flip side, if the competitor is the target of an in-process acquisition, the acquirer may restrict the types of moves the target can make before the deal's completion.

Another common reason for lack of prioritizing a response is that the competitor is in the midst of addressing multiple large problems in their current performance. Again, this is different from problems distracting them from seeing the threat. They may know perfectly well that it's coming but aren't in position to respond because of the precarious position in which they find themselves.

Of course, you're probably thinking, "If they're in so much trouble that they can't prioritize responding to our threatening move, why not just respond to our move and help themselves out of a jam?" It's true that *not* responding to you might create even more problems, but it's a matter of timing. If you are introducing a new product with the potential to capture 15 percent market share in eighteen months, most companies would see that as a big threat. Even if the competitor has 60 percent market share, you've just captured a quarter of their volume— and could possibly continue to do so over the next eighteen months. If they have debt coming due in three months and they're struggling to make the payment, they will almost certainly avoid a fight over market share (which costs money they don't have) in order to stay solvent. The competitor's time frame, not your own, is what matters in terms of their prioritization.

Your communication to the market about your strategic intentions can also influence the competitor's thinking. There is a balancing act between providing enough information so investors will have confidence in your strategy and not giving away so much that competitors will understand the implications to themselves. Strategic communication is especially important for smaller players going up against larger incumbents. As we saw with Eagle Snacks, making it clear they were going to expand into all other distribution channels crystalized for

Frito-Lay that this would affect Frito-Lay's performance outcomes. On the other hand, if Anheuser-Busch had taken a stealthier approach to launching in certain markets and with individual retailers, without any large promotional announcements, it might have been too late for Frito-Lay to respond as aggressively as they did.

If the competitor doesn't even see the move you are planning, they cannot respond to it. If competitors don't feel that your strategic move is going to materially threaten their performance, it's unlikely they'll react and risk overturning the apple cart. And if the competitor has other priorities to address, they can't distract themselves with counteracting your move.

The reality is that companies aren't always aware of the moves you are making—at least not initially. In 2008, I developed a survey with Kevin Coyne that was run through the *McKinsey Quarterly*.[4] The survey asked 1,825 executives about the processes they used to respond to a competitor's major move that occurred in the previous two years. Half the managers were asked to recall reacting to a competitor's major pricing move, while the other half were asked about a retrospective major new product introduction.[5] All the managers were the responders— reacting to the initial move of another organization.

Since the survey asked the executives about major competitive moves they'd faced, we knew these companies had seen the threat. Instead, the executives were asked *when* they had first seen the threat. Forty-four percent of the pricing respondents found out about the pricing moves when they were announced or when they hit the market. A third of the innovation respondents found out when the new product was announced or hit the market. Twenty percent of the pricing moves were not seen until after the pricing change had been on the market, while 13 percent of the innovation moves had a similar delay before the competitor observed them. Is the competitor sitting around, waiting to pounce and kill your strategic move? Not according to the survey: less than one-quarter of the innovation respondents said they were aware of the new product with enough advance notice to have already planned a response before the product was launched. Only one in eight pricing respondents had the same foresight.

In other words, over 75 percent of the time, your competitor won't see the threat with enough warning to counteract your move before it hits the market. You don't have to worry that they are waiting to attack your new strategy upon its launch, but you do have to worry about what they'll do after you execute the new strategy. Assuming they will see, feel, and prioritize your threat, what will they do next?

What Will They Consider?

To predict what your competitor will do, now that you're sure they'll do something, you have to start by thinking about the set of choices they'll consider. Game theory, which is the study of strategic interactions between players, offers us some insight. Game theory has five critical building blocks for defining the game at hand:

- The list of participants (who are the players?)
- Their objectives (what do they want?)
- The strategic options (what can they do?)
- The information about the game—including the game's rules (what do they know?)
- The payoffs (what do they get?)

We're focused on the third element: the strategic options. Game theory tells us to consider all viable choices a player *could* make in the game, whether they actually use those choices or not. For the sake of completeness, this is a fabulous way to approach the problem. By considering every possible option, you will be certain to leave no stone unturned. You will assess every potential choice and make sure you've thought through each contingency outcome of the different selections.

In reality, this simply isn't feasible. Game theorists recognize this and typically reduce the number of strategies to a manageable set, with the trade-off of simplifying the game they are playing. In the real world, you have to face all the complex messiness. That's what this whole book is about. Don't simplify the competitor's choices down to what you want them to do. Think about the world from their perspective and consider it from their viewpoint. But this seems to return us to the same problem: they could do almost anything, so how can we assess the set of choices they will consider?

The good news is that, while in theory we have to consider all their possible choices, in practice competitor organizations are composed of human beings who take shortcuts and simplify their world when under time pressure. And make no mistake, when you introduce a major strategic move and the competitor sees, feels, and prioritizes the threat, the clock starts ticking. Look at it from the competitor's viewpoint: the manager in charge goes to talk with the CEO to tell her that you (their competitor) have just launched a new pricing scheme, launched a new service, or entered a new market. The manager says he expects the move to have a negative impact on his performance. Will the CEO say, "Hmmm, that's interesting. Why don't you take a few months, think of various options, test and assess which one you think is the most viable, syndicate it with the rest of the organization to get buy-in, and then let's attack back"? Or would she say something like "Not now! All right, I need to see your suggested response by the end the week—at the latest!"? Most times, it's the latter.

If your competitor is in a time crunch, they won't have the luxury of coming up with a myriad of potential responses. Neither will they be able to create exotically complex reactions. How do we know? The *McKinsey Quarterly* survey asked the respondents to indicate how many distinct options the organization devoted resources to analyzing—not just the choices or ideas they tossed around but the ones they actually spent time (and money) assessing. A bit less than 10 percent of the respondents said they analyzed only one; they locked onto one idea and started plugging away at it. A third said they spent resources on two different options, while a bit over one-quarter said they looked into three potential reactions. In all, two-thirds of the respondents indicated that they looked at no more than three potential responses.[6]

But which three did they consider? It still seems like an impossible task to understand which three creative options they'll focus on for thwarting your plans. Recall the time pressure though—they don't have the luxury of being able to have off-site brainstorming sessions to craft creative responses. They'll likely reach for some relatively obvious choices and begin assessing them. Once again, the survey bears this out. When asked what types of reactions they considered, the most common response was "the single most obvious counteraction," with 55 percent of respondents selecting this answer. The survey didn't ask for details on what that reply meant, but since it was asking for how the respondent, as a competitor, reacted to a pricing or new product introduction, we can interpret that selection in a couple of ways.

For pricing moves, the most obvious competitor reaction is to match the initial price change. If the company's strategic move is to drop the price by 5 percent, then the obvious counteraction is to drop prices by (about) 5 percent. If the company raises prices by 5 percent, then the obvious counteraction might be to also raise prices by 5 percent. An example of this is the change in pricing structures within the mobile phone industry in the United States. The pricing plans and service levels across the three major players are often remarkably similar. When one moves their price, the others usually respond in the same direction. When the first carrier changed their pricing structures to eliminate two-year contracts that bundled the handset with service, the others followed similarly within a short period of time. In many industries, changes in prices and pricing structures tend to follow each other even when the product or service is not a pure commodity.

For new product introductions, there are two obvious counteractions. First, if the competitor is capable of introducing the same type of product or service, they'll consider reacting with "let's introduce a copycat product." This happens quite often in the financial services industry: when one financial institution introduces a new product, others copy quickly. The second common counteraction is "let's drop our price." If the new product or service is of higher quality, then dropping the price to prevent customers from switching to the new product is a quick and easy reaction to implement.

The key to understanding the "obvious counteraction" lies in looking at the history of moves within your industry, not at what a strategy textbook says to do. How do these types of pricing, entry, or product introduction games typically play out? Do the competitors copy each other? Do they drop prices to prevent customers from switching? Is there a pattern that might not happen 100 percent of the time but gets implemented often enough? Use the historical patterns in your industry as the obvious counteraction.

We've figured out one potential response: the most obvious counteraction. The second and third most common responses differ a bit depending on if the respondents were in the pricing group of executives or the innovation respondent pool. Forty-three percent of the pricing responses considered what the same division within the corporation did the last time they faced a similar pricing move. They thought, "What did we do last time and did it work?" A manager pressed for time will almost certainly try to repeat a past success. For the innovation responses, just over one-quarter of the respondents considered what the same division had previously done. The second most common source of inspiration for the innovation responders was advice from board members or external advisors: "What do consultants say we should do?" Thirty-two percent of the innovation responses claimed this was analyzed, while 30 percent of the pricing respondents assessed this as a reaction.

What do all these numbers and options really mean? If the competitor is most likely to spend time assessing two or three options when considering a response, the top two or three are the following:

1. The most obvious counteraction

2. What the same division did last time

3. What external experts say

You should be able to predict the considered responses to your brilliant strategic move. The most obvious counteraction is what you'd do if faced with the same threat (or what has historically been done in your industry). You can revisit what that same division did previously (because you've cataloged past actions as step 1 of chapter 1's framework). And you can ask your own board members or consultants (if you use them) what they would do in response to your proposed strategic shift. If you don't use consultants, don't worry—I'm not advising that you go out and hire some. Consultants typically offer some variation on the obvious response or prior successful competitor moves (either from your specific competitor or another company). Other than the successful moves of other organizations that are not direct competitors, you've already explored these possible responses.

Four other responses across both the pricing and innovation groups garnered about 20 percent consideration as potential competitive responses. They were what the same division had done "the time before last" (i.e., go back two responses), what a different division within the corporation had done previously when faced with a similar threat, what the executive in charge of deciding this response had done when making a prior choice, and what another company did when faced with the same type of challenge. You don't have to delve into all of these as potential responses, but if you've been doing your four-part process to get inside your competitor's head, you've already covered the first three anyway. What the competitor has done in the past—both in the particular division and across the corporation—*is* the four-step process ("make a prediction and see what happens" implies that you're tracking what they've done). Remember, you should track the implications of the competitor's organizational scope on the division you compete with. What the executive in charge of deciding has done in the past is informed by step 3 (who is deciding?). If you have good insight into the decision maker as an individual, you'll have some background on what she's done in similar situations—or at least which organizations she worked for—so you can figure out what she and they did previously.

But what if the competitor's consultants advised them to look to what others had done in the past from different industries, geographies, and time periods? Or what if they suggested an innovative response that they had seen work in a particular case? Well, at some point, you can't perfectly predict all the possible options the competitor will consider. But remember, that isn't your objective: you want to increase the chance you will think about the potential reactions they *will* explore. Competitors are likely to only explore two or three options when responding. If you can know with a fair amount of certainty six of the top seven sources of potential reactions, you'll have a great chance of predicting what your competitor will analyze as they burn the midnight oil to thwart your move.

What Will They Choose to Do?

Now that you have a good idea of what they will consider as possible responses, you have to ask yourself which one they will actually select. Here, too, the task seems daunting. Sure, we can look to the choices they've made in the past, but as any good investor knows, past performance is not indicative of future results. In other words, there isn't any guarantee they will make the same choice again.

If we look to game theory again for an answer, we can get tripped up if we aren't careful in how we apply the concepts. First off, game theory asserts that players will make a selection among all the possible choices to help achieve the best possible outcome for themselves. If we know what their objective is, we can look at the two or three most likely choices we identified above to determine the optimal selection. This means we have to identify the competitor's objective. Here again, our four-step process comes into play. Step 1 told us to pay attention to what they say. What metrics do they discuss on earnings calls? What do analysts pay attention to in their reports on the company (if publicly traded)? What metrics are discussed in the CEO's letter to shareholders? What lead metrics do they report in press releases?

Combine this with step 3: who is deciding? What metrics are the basis for the senior executives' compensation bonuses? What metrics are reported on by division presidents? If publicly traded, how the corporation reports division-level performance will provide clues to the metrics that matter. What do the division presidents talk about in their press releases? Or what does the CEO say she expects from divisional performance? Home in on the specific metrics the manager who is making the ultimate decision is trying to reach. Remember, we've already considered the relevant metrics: in the first stage of predicting their response, we asked if the competitor would feel the threat based on the metrics she must reach.

The *McKinsey Quarterly* survey asked about the primary performance metric used to evaluate the potential choices. Contrary to what most people assume, only 6 (pricing) or 7 (innovation) percent of respondents used the net present value (NPV) of their possible reactions to make a choice. Another 7 (pricing) to 9 (innovation) percent calculated the NPV of the reaction plus some expected benefit from discouraging future strategic moves by other competitors (i.e., making others think twice about trying something as bold as what you did). Overall, no more than 15 percent of the respondents aimed for maximizing NPV.

What do competitors look at instead? Most often, innovation moves are considered in light of their impact on market share, while pricing moves are evaluated according to their impact on earnings or cash flow. In addition, competitors do not focus on a long timeframe. Almost 50 percent of innovation responses used forecasts six to twenty-four months into the future, while 60 percent of the pricing reactions did the same. These were not long-term assessments, which makes sense if you think about it. A manager tasked with responding to a major competitive move will want to make sure she performs well enough to keep her job. After two years, the employee feedback cycle will probably not incorporate information on her particular response. If you want to survive and advance in your role, you better make sure to perform well in the next couple of years—more so than worrying about what happens five or six years out.

The second way game theory helps is with thinking through the dynamic reactions. Because you're making a strategic change and then your competitor is responding, you'll be able to respond again, which they can then react to, which creates another reply from you, and so on. This is called *multiround sequential game theory*: each round is a choice, and players make those choices in sequence one after the other. Here, game theory advises you to think about all the potential reactions and countermoves, but it gets daunting to play this out over the course of several choices. (Wasn't part of the struggle trying to determine the competitor's first reaction, and now we're trying to figure out their third, fourth, and fifth responses?!)

Again, the survey reveals you don't have to worry about thinking that far ahead. Approximately one-quarter of all respondents stated they didn't even model in one counteraction by the company making the first move. In other words, they spent time and resources figuring out how to respond, but they didn't think it would matter how the original company would react! Another 35 to 40 percent modeled in only one further reaction move (either by the original company or another competitor). Only 20–25 percent of the time did the competitor create a multiround game of moves and countermoves.

Competitors don't have the luxury of creating and evaluating complex, multiround game theoretic models, which means you don't have to assume they are. Model their potential response (the second move after your initial strategic change) based on what provides them with the best outcome according to their goals and objectives—likely shorter-term earnings or market share. What would you do in reaction to that move (the third move in sequence)? Will your reaction change their prior move (the second one) to a different response? Answering these simple questions will almost certainly replicate their analysis and provide a good sense of what your competitor will do.

There is one more consideration regarding your competitor's reaction: will they overcome their own internal organizational inertia in order to respond? Just because the competitor has done the analysis and made a choice doesn't mean the organization will actually implement the reaction. This is different from prioritizing the threat (which we covered in the first key question). That original point concerned the competitor actually spending time exploring available options to make a choice. Here, the leadership has prioritized the threat and decided the best mode of reaction but ultimately can't move the organization to act. Innovation is a perfect example: larger companies often have a more difficult time creating an innovative environment than smaller start-up companies do. If an entrepreneur develops a new product that revolutionizes the sector, the competitor's leadership may decide that copying the product (or coming up with an even better one) is their best response. But it may not be possible to convince the R&D staff to drop what they're doing to copy the entrepreneur ("Where's the excitement in that? It's not creative or new . . .") or come up with a brand-new product ("I've spent three years perfecting this product that's almost ready to take to market, and you want me to drop it to come up with something different?"). Unless the R&D staff buy into the new model and commit to changing their focus, an effective response will not be implemented.

You probably recognize that this inertia conundrum is informed by step 3 of chapter 1's framework: who must change their behavior, and are they incentivized to do so? Will the frontline staff implement what the senior leaders want? If not, there's less likelihood the competitor will respond. This is what 17 percent, or approximately one in six, of the survey respondents ultimately ended up doing. They spent time analyzing the potential responses to a major competitive move but ended up doing nothing.

Predicting Reactions for Any Type of Competitor

It might appear that the three-stage set of key questions only applies to publicly held companies, but these questions can be asked of any organization. Will it matter to a nonprofit that an alternative organization just launched a new campaign to raise €10,000,000? Will the nonprofit even be aware of the fundraising effort? Will the campaign threaten their sources of funding or ability to partner with others to execute their own mission? And will they prioritize responding over other efforts they're undertaking?

What options will a privately held company consider? Probably a very similar list to what we've described above: an obvious counteraction, what they did last time, or what a trusted advisor might suggest. The middle option of these—what they did last time—might even be more common in a privately held company. Strong ownership (family or individual) at the top will tend to repeat past successful actions. Use insights developed from chapter 1, step 3 to ascertain the leaders' behavioral patterns.

The final question—how will they decide what to do?—is analyzed identically with regard to the number of rounds and back-and-forth reactions they'll consider. The difference is that the competitor might try to achieve alternative objectives. Instead of earnings and market share (and possibly NPV), a nonprofit will look at metrics such as fundraising goals, the number of individuals served, or the percentage decrease in a particular disease, depending on the mission they support. Use chapter 1, step 1 here. Pay attention to the nonprofit's mission statement or to what the leaders say about their fundraising objectives (e.g., amounts of money, sources to tap, special campaigns).

A privately held company might have longer-term objectives in mind, while a family-owned company where the matriarch is nearing retirement might have other objectives, such as determining who will take over the organization. This succession challenge might lead to shorter-term objectives, with different siblings attempting to prove their division is better, and therefore they should lead the entire organization. (This in-fighting might also mean your move doesn't matter to them; they might not see your move or prioritize the threat, so there wouldn't be a reaction to analyze.)

Finally, if you want to understand how a government regulator might react, their interests could include things such as expanding the agency's budget or proving their toughness in order to retain their position. They might be influenced because the administration is nearing the end of its term and the agency head wants to leave a legacy (or because the incumbent politician wants to increase the chances of her party's reelection).

As we saw in chapter 2, there are two sides to the coin when thinking about entrepreneurs. Start-up companies must think about how incumbents will react to them. Additionally, incumbents must consider whether, and how, an entrepreneur will respond. This process is critically important for entrepreneurs considering incumbents' reactions. An entrepreneur is most likely entering a market where incumbents already are serving customers. Just as Anheuser-Busch had to consider Frito-Lay's reaction when they expanded into grocery and convenience stores, a start-up has to think about the reaction of incumbents to the entrepreneur's entry into the market. If an entrepreneur introduces a product that will only serve a niche part of the market and doesn't plan to expand further (and this plan is well understood by the incumbents), then the new entrant likely won't matter to the existing players.

However, if those incumbents fear the entrant will expand, it *will* matter. The existing companies will consider reactions that will probably include objectives such as containing the entrant to a small portion of the market or trying to prevent them from gaining a foothold in the first place. Regardless, the entrepreneur can walk through the three key questions in this chapter to assess if the incumbents think the entrant matters to them, what responses they'll consider, and which one they'll choose. One critically important element for the entrepreneur is how to communicate their intentions to the market. A start-up must balance the desire to fly low enough under the radar of the large incumbents to avoid a harsh response while at the same time growing large enough to attract venture funding. Remaining a niche player means less chance of an incumbent's response, but it also means the company will be less attractive to investors.

As far as an incumbent's consideration of how an entrepreneur might respond to that incumbent's initiative, your initial thought may be "who cares?" The incumbent is bigger than the entrepreneur, has more resources, and can easily "squash" the start-up if desired (all within the limits of the relevant anticompetitive laws). The risk here is an entrepreneur who offers a competing product or service that is superior to the incumbent's new or existing offering. Once the incumbent has staked out their market position, a smaller, nimbler entrepreneur can pivot to differentiate themselves from the incumbent. For example, the entrepreneur can seek out customers who are underserved by the incumbent's new initiative and serve them better and then use that base to grow into a broader offering. If the incumbent is concerned about this happening (especially if they are launching a new strategic initiative that is entrepreneurial itself), then they absolutely need to think about how a smaller entrepreneur might derail their new strategy.

Again, the three questions present us with some insights. It is quite possible that the start-up will not be able to prioritize the incumbent's threat. For example, the entrepreneur could be completely absorbed with making sure their own venture doesn't fail. (They might not even see the threat posed by the incumbent's new strategic move in the first place.) The start-up doesn't have the same track record of previous moves to rely on for determining which options they might consider, but there are places to look for clues, listed below.

- What did the entrepreneur's previous companies do? The founders' past experience will be a good indication of the types of strategic moves they will consider (as we saw in chapter 1, step 3).

- What *can* the entrepreneur do? What resources are they drawing on? What functional experience does the leadership team possess? In which geographic markets do they have a presence? Once again, chapter 1 proves helpful (steps 2 and 3).

- What is the entrepreneur's objective? Though it's hard to know with certainty, it's probably best to start with "short-term survival." Most start-ups are not yet at a point where they can reasonably think about long-term earnings or market share. When push comes to shove, they'll probably choose an option maximizing their chance to make it through the next quarter and year. For example, they might survive only by making a defensive move in response to the incumbent or pivoting into a new geography or customer segment to avoid the incumbent's new move.

What if the incumbent is thinking about how an unknown, not-yet-launched entrepreneur might take advantage of their initiative? Then we're back to chapter 1's framework: what resources would be needed to defeat this initiative and what kind of leader—with what kind of background—would that require? The incumbent should be on the lookout for companies with these kinds of profiles. Admittedly, this is a difficult task, but using this thought experiment could actually lead the incumbent to generating new ideas for their own initiatives by framing the challenge from a different perspective.

The three questions apply to all types of organizations. Your competitors still have to feel like your move matters to them before they will explore doing something about it. They will select a handful of options to analyze (because they don't have the luxury of time) and will pick the one that best helps their own organization achieve its objectives. If you can answer these three key questions, you'll be in a great position to predict your competitor's response.

A chess player who ignores thinking about potential reactions to their moves will often find their queen trapped and their king soon checkmated. You can avoid the same fate in business by thinking a few moves ahead of your competitor. The good news is they aren't playing three-dimensional chess—they're generally not engaging in highly creative strategies that are beyond your grasp. You can forecast what they will likely do and avoid walking into a trap.

4 Are They Getting Ready to Pounce on Us?

There are multiple examples of movies with the same essential plot coming out in the same year:

- *Volcano* and *Dante's Peak* in 1997, about the impending doom of a volcanic eruption
- *Armageddon* and *Deep Impact* in 1998, about projectiles from outer space on a collision course with Earth
- *Antz* and *A Bug's Life* in 1998, about anthropomorphic animated insects battling to save their way of life
- *Red Planet* and *Mission to Mars* in 2000, about trying to survive in the harsh environs of the planet Mars, where potential disaster is always right around the corner

The challenge with these movies for each of the production companies involved real uncertainty (if not mortal danger): would the theater-going public be interested in this particular story, especially considering that a nearly exact duplicate movie would be coming out in the same year?

It takes years to develop, film, and then release a movie. While it's true that information about scripts is known within the industry at an early development stage, the timing of when the movie will be filmed (i.e., when it will raise enough funding) is not clear. Production companies struggle with the question of whether their competitors are going to beat them to the punch and release a movie before they do. And at the earliest stages, they have to wonder if that great new script they read will be trumped at its release date by a competitor's movie around the same time.

This question is often on the minds of companies in other sectors as they think about what their competitors are planning. Is it worth even trying to predict your competitors' next move, or should you merely react to moves they make when they are revealed? The previous chapter showed how competitors react, but it is also important to contemplate their potential proactive moves coming your way in the near future— the second challenge we raised at the beginning of the previous chapter.

A different set of three questions can help you assess the likelihood that your competitors are in the process of revisiting their strategy and are about to make an adjustment. Let's examine each of these in turn, buttressed by the results of a second survey conducted through the *McKinsey Quarterly*, again developed with Kevin Coyne.[1] In this one, we asked companies about the process they went through for the largest strategic initiative their business unit undertook in the previous five years. The 1,552 responses were not in reaction to a competitive move (which the previous survey explored) but were "spontaneous" strategic moves. As we'll see below, not all of the responses are what one would expect, but all of them provide insight for predicting whether your competitor is preparing to launch a new strategy.

Question #1: Are They Ripe for a Change?

The obvious place to start is to try and determine whether the competitor needs a new strategic direction. Every organization shifts their focus over time and for different reasons. By thinking through several reasons why an organization might make a strategic change, you can understand if these conditions apply to your competitor.

Do Internal Factors Point to a Reassessment?

One reason a company might be ready to make a strategic shift is because their old strategy has fully played out. They may have achieved everything they planned to accomplish with their existing strategy and now need to shift. This is often seen with branding campaigns: companies will refresh their brand, not necessarily because of a scandal involving their previous name or logo but because they want to rein-vigorate their positioning in customers' minds.

Change can also occur with broader strategic shifts. An interesting perspective on this comes from research by Peter Boumgarden, Jackson Nickerson, and Todd Zenger.[2] They found that while some companies can both search for new ideas and execute on those new ideas at the same time (being ambidextrous), many companies have to switch back and forth between creating organizational structures to explore new opportunities and those that allow them to exploit those new strate-gies (vacillation). For competitors that are vacillators, observe whether they've recently been structured to explore (decentralized, focused on experimentation) or exploit (centralized, focused on operational execu-tion and efficiency). A long length of time in one of the positions can be a good indicator that they may be ready to tack their sailboat in a new direction. (The authors use that metaphor to describe organiza-tions that vacillate: they go "north" by heading northwest, tack back northeast, and then return to a northwestern direction, etc.) Our survey provides some evidence for how often this is the case. Only 19 percent of the respondents indicated their previous strategy had run its course and their business unit needed a new direction.

New leadership may be another reason the competitor is ready to make a strategic realignment. A new CEO will often build their own C-suite executive team and formulate a new strategy.[3] This is especially true for "outsider" CEOs who come from a different organization: part of the reason they are hired is that the board of directors wants the company to go in a different direction.[4] The Conference Board found that in 2020, 33 percent of the incoming CEOs at Russell 3000 compa-nies were outsiders, while it was 25 percent for S&P 500 successions.[5] "Insider" CEOs can also change the company's strategic direction, but that will often happen if they have a different functional background from the previous CEO (e.g., a chief financial officer (CFO) or chief operating officer (COO) getting promoted can indicate a shift toward efficiency and a chief marketing officer (CMO) toward marketing and product innovation).

Our survey indicates that 10 percent of the time, new *corporate* leaders wanted to change the business unit's strategic direction, while another 9 percent of the time new *business unit* leaders initiated the shift in strategy. This should seem very reminiscent of step 3 from chapter 1 because it is! Pay attention to the new leader and their background, and then assess the implications for an impending strategic shift. The survey results support paying attention to your competitors' senior leaders: 73 percent of the time the CEO or COO authorized the search for a new strategy, while another 8 percent of the time it was a different C-suite executive. An additional 11 percent responded that the search was directed by the head of a business unit or division. In total, 92 percent of the time the search for a new strategy was authorized by the C-suite or divisional presidents (and overwhelmingly the CEO or COO). You know who to pay attention to: the senior leaders of the competition. If they start talking about strategic change, or if there's high turnover in their ranks, you should be ready for them to adjust course.

Does Their Performance Indicate They Need a Change?

When a company is struggling and not meeting their financial and other strategic performance goals, it's natural to think they would be questioning their strategy. In times of trouble, when things aren't heading in the right direction, a change seems warranted. However, this is a situation where the survey results are a bit of a mixed bag. On the one hand, 29 percent of the respondents indicated that the business unit changed strategic direction because the previous strategy was not meeting its objectives and the company wanted a new direction. This was the most common rationale indicated. (Approximately 10 percent of the participants answered this question because they actually undertook a new strategic direction). On the other hand, across all the survey participants, which included those who continued in the same direction or in a slightly different strategic direction, 30 percent of respondents said they were underperforming on financial targets, one-third were meeting financial targets, and another third were outperforming their targets before they considered the new strategic initiative (the other 3 percent answered "don't know"). Over 70 percent of the outperformers reported outcomes at least 5 percent above their targets, which is really good performance!

As expected, those who reported that the previous strategy was not effective also reported underperforming on their financial targets, while those significantly outperforming reported their strategy had run its course. The CEO or COO was most often cited as the impetus for strategic changes across all performance levels (between 61 percent and 83 percent of the responses), although if the divisional heads were tasked with leading the new strategic search, it was most likely to occur if the company was underperforming (almost 20 percent of responses if the company was underperforming, while only 9 percent if outperforming).

Why is this the case? The best explanation is that the best performers have the luxury of time to think about big, corporate-wide strategic shifts, while those who are struggling will more likely look to divisional heads to turn things around. It may feel obvious that a company facing challenges will change course, but they may be so busy putting out fires and preventing the whole thing from collapsing that they don't have the time or space to be strategic. They're reactive, not proactive.

Another potential driver of these results is that outperformers have a current competitive advantage that allows these superior results, and they are actively searching for the next competitive advantage to maintain their lead. We asked what initiated the new strategic direction: an opportunity that presented itself, an active search, or a challenge that necessitated a response. The highest outperformers were more likely to respond to opportunities (43 percent as opposed to 31 percent of the worst performers) and were more likely to actively search (34 versus 26 percent). Underperformers were more likely to respond to challenges (38 to 22 percent). When you're in the lead, you have the space to seek out new options or to be aware of opportunities that arise.

Did an External (or Internal) Stimulus Appear?
The final consideration for whether your competitor is ripe for a change is the appearance of any stimuli that would "force" them to

reorient their strategy. Examples of external stimuli could include the following:

- a change in regulatory policy that opens up a new market that was previously blocked
- a shift in customer preference that makes the competitor's products more desirable
- the availability of new technology that connects their services with existing products or services
- a change in geopolitical conditions

The last example demonstrates these external stimuli could be either positive or negative. For example, a country opening its economy to imports provides an opportunity to begin selling products or services into that country. On the other hand, if a country decides to impose new restrictions on certain trading partners, then a company from that trading partner may decide to shift their strategy to outsource more production to avoid those restrictions. Similarly, customers may shift their preferences *away* from the competitor, technology may make their solutions obsolete, or other regulatory policies may create headwinds. Our survey indicated that 17 percent of the respondents felt that external conditions changed such that their old strategy was going to be less effective, hence necessitating a change. Twelve percent reported that changing external conditions created even better strategic opportunities.

These external stimuli should be relatively easy to track because your company needs to be aware of the same types of effects. If technological, customer, or political shifts occur, they will probably affect you too. These stimuli need to be on your radar already, but they might have a greater impact on your competitors. If they are paying attention to them, the shocks may generate an impetus to shift their strategy.

Internal stimuli, on the other hand, are much harder to track. One example of an internal stimulus to seek a new strategy could be the integration of a new acquisition. The deal itself could be a strategic shift the company decided to undertake (either in reaction to a move by your organization or spontaneously), but once the deal closes, the hard work of integration begins. The acquisition could be for purely financial gain, but it could also have a strategic element: helping to lower costs or generate additional revenue through synergies between the two organizations. An internal stimulus to seek and exploit synergies has a clear precursor—and one you can observe (since it's often a rationale in the deal announcement).

Other possible internal stimuli (besides changing leadership, which we've discussed above) include resolutions of legal proceedings (e.g., patent lawsuits), new joint ventures, or a change in financial structure (e.g., change in debt/equity ratio). One way to track these big internal stimuli is to pay attention to press releases or filings with regulatory agencies, especially for publicly traded companies. Material changes that must be reported could indicate a potential shift in strategic direction.

Tracking if your competitor has internal factors pointing toward strategic reassessment, if their performance is conducive to a strategic shift, or if external stimuli exist can provide you with a better sense for whether the conditions are right for your competitor to seek a new strategy. These conditions could lead to the competitor searching for a new strategy (because they have the luxury of time) or responding to an opportunity or challenge (because of internal or external stimuli). In our survey, we found that 29 percent of respondents said they actively conducted a search for a new strategy, while 41 percent responded to an opportunity and 27 percent to a challenge. While these results seem relatively evenly split between the three options, we can view them as revealing that two-thirds of the time companies were developing new strategies in reactions to stimuli (positive or negative) in their environment. As highlighted above, these are occurrences you can often track, so don't be completely surprised when they lead to new competitor moves.

Question #2: What Is Their Likely Direction?

To figure out which strategic direction the competitor might take, one of the first issues the survey can help with is predicting how different the new strategic direction will be. It's natural to think your competitor is sitting on a brand-new strategy that is a 180-degree shift from their current strategy—one which will completely throw off all their current competitors and leave them in the dust. But when we asked the survey participants to categorize the nature of the new strategic direction they took, 85 percent said it was in addition to their current strategy! Most often, the competitor's brilliant new strategy doesn't replace their current strategy—it runs alongside it. This is important for two reasons. First, it means the competitor will not be fully focused on the new idea—it's likely not a "bet the company" initiative. Second, it means the new strategy will likely be somewhat aligned with the existing strategy, making it easier to predict the direction they'll head.

Support for this second conclusion comes from the survey respondents: 61 percent stated the new strategy continued in the same direction the business unit had been going the previous three years. An additional 34 percent stated they went in a different direction though not a reversal. Only 4 percent indicated the new strategy reversed the company's historical direction. The competition are not zigzagging back and forth—at worst they are tacking (as in the vacillation versus ambidexterity research above) or merely continuing downwind.

There are questions you can ask yourself to better assess the path the competitor might take if the new strategy isn't a continuation of their existing strategic direction. The questions will be similar to the ones asked in previous chapters though with a slightly different focus.

Is There a Strong Pattern from the Decision Maker?

Similar to chapter 1's step 3, you want to understand who the competitor's decision maker is. Most often, it will be the CEO or COO, and many companies have detailed profiles of these senior executives on their websites. Gather information on the decision maker's past choices: what kinds of strategies did they implement or manage in their previous roles? If the strategies were successful, they will likely be considered strongly again. (After all, the plans worked because of the brilliance of the senior executive, didn't they?[6]) Recall the results from chapter 3's survey: competitors recycle options that worked before. Even if they were unsuccessful strategies, the leader may still decide to try them again because the failure must not have been their fault.

How Many Choices Will They Explore?

The more choices that are considered, the more difficult it will be to figure out which one will be selected. Approximately 50 percent of the time, competitors devote resources to evaluating one or two options when selecting their strategy regardless of whether it's a response to an opportunity/challenge or a proactive search. About 8 percent of the time they'll evaluate four or more options when responding to an opportunity/challenge, while that percentage jumps to 14 percent when they are proactively seeking a new strategy. These numbers should make sense—instead of spending a lot of time evaluating dozens of different ideas, companies explore just a few. If they took the time and resources to analyze more options, they might be too late to take advantage of the emerging opportunity, or the challenge might quickly overwhelm them. Even proactive searching can lead to "paralysis by analysis," though the luxury of not being pressured by external stimuli does give companies a slightly greater chance of casting their net more widely for ideas.

As we saw with competitive reactions, companies don't explore the plethora of options they theoretically could. Even when spontaneously crafting a new strategy, executives need to answer to the CEO or the board. Neither will sit around for long waiting for the "perfect" solution. As we'll see in the next section, the timing of the strategic action creates some of the pressure influencing a smaller set of options.

Are There Environmental Cues?

The final dimensions influencing potential strategic directions come from the external environment. Are customers changing the types of products or services they demand? Have certain geographies created new opportunities or challenges? Are there specific customer groups that have changed their buying patterns and habits and become a natural segment the competitor might pursue? These dimensions can either be positive for the competitor (i.e., opening up obvious avenues on which to focus) or negative (i.e., ones the competitor will shift away from and avoid).

When thinking about these environmental cues, ask yourself whether the new focal points reinforce the competitor's historical patterns or if they push them to alter their usual choices. Again, answer these questions for both the organization overall and the specific decision maker at that organization. (If the specific decision maker is unknown, use the CEO or business unit head as a proxy.) If their historical strategic patterns are reinforced by these environmental factors, then the chance they will consider pursing those opportunities increases (the familiar is always an enticing option). But if your competitor needs to shift how they operate or pursue areas in which they have no experience, then those options will fall lower on the list to consider. This doesn't imply they will or will not choose those options—that is the subject of the next section. But if the competitor is only going to consider one or two options, and two obvious options that fit their historical patterns open up in their immediate market segment, then those two should rise to the top of the list for consideration.

Question #3: What Tactics Will They Choose?

We will diverge slightly from the advice in the previous chapter on predicting your competitor's reaction, where we focused on the decision-making objective. The competitor's goal is important to consider as you think about which option they will choose. But in some sense, when planning a spontaneous strategic move—one not made in response to competitors—the same or similar evaluation criteria will likely be used. In most cases, competitors will focus on longer-term metrics like profitability. (Not always—again, look for historical patterns: if the competitor always pursues market share first, use that as the evaluation metric.) In this case, we'll focus on four different dimensions along which competitors will make their decision.

How Quickly Will They Make a Change (and What Will It Look Like When They Do)?

The first point to consider is *when* they might make their move. Will this happen in the next few weeks, in which case you will be playing catch-up? Or will it take them several months to execute, in which case you can start to prepare some general plans, modifying them as needed once you know the exact form their strategy takes?

With regard to the timing, there are four important subdimensions to consider. For each, we have supporting evidence from our survey. The first is when the planning occurs, the second is the length of time from beginning a search until a decision to proceed is made, the third is how long it takes from decision to implementation, and the fourth is the implementation process.

When They Make Their Plans   Many companies engage in an annual strategic planning process. There are good reasons to have a set process and many bad reasons to stick to it. (Books are written on this topic alone, so we won't delve into it further.[7]) But for our purposes, we want to know if companies use annual processes to create new, spontaneous strategic shifts or whether they typically result from ad hoc committees. We found that 54 percent of the time, it's the strategic planning process that carries the day, while 32 percent of the time shifts are made on an ad hoc basis outside of the strategic planning process. This is nearly a two-to-one advantage. Most companies have a strategic planning process that occurs in the latter part of the fiscal year (to set up the coming fiscal year's budgets). As your competitor nears the time for their strategic planning process, you can begin to think about the likelihood they will feel pressured to make a switch.

Those good at math will realize we've only accounted for 86 percent of the responses. Another 10 percent reported they created their new strategy on an ad hoc basis because they didn't have an annual strategic planning process. I have chosen not to lump these in with the 32 percent mentioned above because this 10 percent of respondents are following their "normal" procedure to assess their strategy. Their planning process isn't on a fixed schedule but neither is it an unusual process for them. Another filter should be applied to these competitors: what is their typical cycle for making changes? If they have historically implemented changes every three years, then look to year three as the time they are liable to develop their next move.

How Long It Takes to Search for the Right Strategy   It sometimes feels like the competitor has developed a new strategy overnight, but often that's because we haven't paid attention to the clues and signals they have given off along the way. If we had tracked the competitor more closely, we would have uncovered indications they were planning something new. But how much time would we have to gather these clues? According to the survey, we would have between six months and a year. Only 3 percent of the 440 respondents who actively searched for a new strategy (as opposed to responding to an opportunity or challenge) spent less than one month on the search process before deciding on the next strategy. Almost half the respondents spent up to six months, while another 26 percent spent seven to twelve months. One in six even reported that they took more than one full year to decide what to do next. The bottom line is that you can figure out what decision the competitor is nearing because you'll have time to gather enough clues—if you are paying attention to them.

How Long Implementation Will Take   Even if it takes several months for the competitor to decide (which makes sense since new strategic shifts are often part of a strategic planning process), they might still surprise you with the actual launch. They could capture a relatively large market share so quickly that you have no time to respond. Our survey tells us, though, you do have time to track what they're doing—if you are paying attention!

After the decision had been made, 31 percent of our respondents took between six months and a year to implement the strategy. It didn't matter if they were responding to an opportunity or a challenge or were actively searching for a new strategy. Another 31 percent indicated it took between one and five years to implement their decision, and 1 percent even reported taking *more* than five years. On the shorter side, about one in eight reported implementing the strategy within three months of making the decision. (Professional services and financial institutions reported executing in the three-month window more often than high tech and manufacturing. Interestingly, the industry that responded most often to having taken more than five years to implement was financial services, so there seems to be a wide variation in the sector's ability to implement new strategies.)

How They Will Go about Implementing It   The final element affecting your ability to forecast your competitor's strategic shift with enough time to prepare a response before it affects your organization is determining the method they'll use to launch the new strategy. If they launch nationally (or globally), it will be hard to respond. However, if they launch incrementally, with market tests and rollouts across regions as the idea proves itself, you will have more time to validate your assessment of their new strategy and if it conforms to their actions.

Overall, the survey indicates that the former—full-out launch into the market—is not the preferred method. While it was the second most selected choice, by 23 percent of the respondents, that execution plan was dwarfed by the other 66 percent who reported a rollout implementation. If you haven't been paying attention to the competitors and aren't assessing what they might do, these slower rollouts may seem surprising. But if you are tracking their potential moves, you won't feel as threatened by them and their moves won't feel like a sudden introduction. In particular, 34 percent of the respondents reported they steadily rolled out the new strategy across segments, 15 percent used small market tests across segments, and 14 percent announced their plans to the entire potential market before launching. Interestingly, 3 percent launched with small market tests, withdrew from the market to analyze the results, and then retested to gain further information. Any of these implementation sequences will give you time to recognize and assess the impact the new strategy will have on you. You can try to rely on third-party publication reports of these moves, but they'll likely be too late by the time they are published. The best way to make sure you are aware of these rollouts is to implement a strong competitive insight function that tracks these types of competitor moves, which will be the topic of chapter 7.

There's one caveat to consider: you should ask if the anticipated competitor strategy can only succeed within a small window of opportunity (e.g., because of impending regulatory changes, upcoming elections, potential acquisitions). If so, you need to assess whether that means the competitor won't consider the move (because it's too brief an opportunity) or if it means they will take the plunge, in which case their strategic shift will come sooner than you might expect otherwise.

How Large an Initiative Will They Implement?

The second dimension that affects the competitor's ultimate choice is the potential size of the new strategic initiative. As you start to narrow in on the potential strategy you think they might choose, ask yourself how big of an investment would be required. Will it be an incremental investment to the assets and resources they already have, or will a completely new infrastructure be required? You don't have to be extraordinarily specific with the estimate—just enough to compare it to your competitor's basic financials. What share of annual revenue does the initiative represent? How does it compare to their market cap? How would this change their outstanding debt? (You could even look at short- versus long-term debt and choose the one that aligns with the length of time the new strategy could play out.) If these ratios seem really big, especially compared to the size of some of their past initiatives, you should be more skeptical about whether the projected strategy will be chosen.

Relatedly, our survey offers some indication of how often companies move beyond their current budgets in order to implement strategic shifts—in other words, how often they'll "bet the farm" on new initiatives. The most common way new strategies were reported to have been financed was that the budget was allocated at the time the decision was made, as indicated by 34 percent of the survey participants. The budget allocation occurred through the normal strategic planning process. Recall from above that a little over half the time the strategic planning process generated the search for new ideas. The formalized process doesn't always result in the necessary budget being allocated, but it's a good estimate to begin with: if they're going through a strategic planning exercise, they'll likely allocate a budget amount to their decision at the same time. Look at the company's prior public announcements about how much they're planning to spend on certain types of activities (like marketing, capital budgeting), and then use those public budget revelations as upper bounds on how much they can allocate to the new strategy. Another 26 percent of survey respondents indicated the necessary funding was found within the existing budget once the decision was made. Combined with the first result, over half the time companies are working within existing budgetary frameworks when allocating funds to the new strategy.

Only 27 percent of the executives reported that money was added to the existing budget to cover the new project. In other words, companies seek additional funding to implement a new strategic direction only about one-quarter of the time. Instead, the norm is that big strategic bets are typically made within the existing financial structure. We tend to think that if the NPV is greater than the hurdle rate (the minimum rate of return a project needs to generate in order to be approved), the company can raise capital from the markets to pay for the project. Our survey indicates this isn't the typical mindset of companies. Remember, the survey asked about the biggest strategic initiative the business unit undertook in the previous five years—major strategic changes, not small bolt-ons. These are exactly the types of moves that should justify raising capital if they meet the organization's hurdle rate. Instead, we found that companies are more likely to stick with existing funding sources. In fact, 6 percent of the respondents reported that the implementation of this big new strategic initiative was delayed until funds could be allocated during the next budgeting cycle. The company waited to execute their new strategic direction until they could fit it within the existing planning process!

Sticking to existing processes and procedures, even when seeking to change the strategic direction, indicates potential risk aversion on the part of most companies. This is our third dimension to explore.

What Is the Typical Risk Appetite of the Decision Maker?

Previously, we've assessed the financial implications for the competitor. Now we want to consider the risk inherent in the potential choices and how they align with the competitor's risk preferences. As always, make sure you are looking at the riskiness from the viewpoint of the other organization—not your organization's risk preferences.

For example, say you think the best play for the competitor would be to build out a multichannel distribution infrastructure for capturing retail consumer-packaged goods growth in India. If the competitor in question has built similar distribution systems in China, Indonesia, and Southeast Asia, then expanding into India wouldn't be that risky, especially compared to another company that only has a presence in Western Europe. The greater the degrees of difference (e.g., along customer segments, geographies, operational structures, capabilities required, political/regulatory processes), the greater the risk involved for the competitor (on top of the financial risk we've discussed above).

Examine the previous risks the competitor has taken with its strategic initiatives. Have they involved "sticking to their knitting," or have there been moves into adjacencies? How closely have those adjacent moves been to their core business? Evaluate the risk preferences of the business unit's and the company's leadership, especially if they came from another sector. Are those other industries populated with more risk-seeking firms? Was the leader's previous company considered a risk-averse organization?

The payback period of the initiative is one measure of the potential riskiness of the strategic move. The longer it takes for the initiative to pay back the investment, the greater the risk that it will never generate a return. While it's hard to assess when the actual payoff will occur for a specific competitor move, use a back-of-the-envelope calculation of what it would take if you were making the investment—how long would it take you to pay it back? (Adjust for the different resources, assets, and capabilities the competitor has relative to you.)

Our survey provides evidence for how risky a company's strategic initiatives are based on the expected payback. Remember, we asked for the biggest strategic move that the business unit had made in the past five years, so they were not small, riskless efforts. Forty-two percent of the respondents indicated a one- to three-year payback period; this could be considered a moderately risky investment. Another 17 percent expected a six- to twelve-month payback, and 5 percent expected the payback period to be less than six months. Overall, almost two-thirds expected to pay back the investment on their largest strategic initiative in less than three years. Of the riskier moves, 21 percent expected payoffs within three to five years, while 9 percent anticipated needing more than five years to pay off the initial investment.

Are There "Typical" Levers They Pull?

The final dimension to consider when assessing the competitor's potential choice is whether there are typical actions they gravitate toward. As we discussed in chapter 1, senior leaders tend to fall back on the habits and patterns that got them to their current position. Similar tendencies occur within companies too: organizations tend to reinforce certain functions, which leads to hiring executives with expertise in those areas, which leads to more focus on those functional areas. Think about the typical moves you've seen from the competitor and from those who will be leading the competitor's potential strategic initiative.

In the survey, we asked about the nature of the strategic initiative selected, and almost one-third of respondents (31 percent) indicated it was a major product innovation (i.e., a new product or service introduced to the immediate market segment, or a modification of an existing offering). New market entry was the second most common move (at 22 percent), followed by merger or acquisition (15 percent), capacity increases or decreases (15 percent), price restructuring (6 percent), and divestiture (4 percent). This spread is to be expected, but there were a few interesting industry deviations from these general results. Business services were more likely to focus on new product innovation and market entry and less on M&As. Financial services were much less likely to try product innovation (it's a copycat industry) but were more likely to enter new markets or engage in transactions (especially divestitures). High tech and telecom were the most likely to try product innovation and the least likely to engage in capacity shifts (probably because of the existing outsourcing opportunities) and were slightly more likely to engage in M&A than the overall pool. Finally, manufacturing sector respondents were less likely to innovate and slightly more likely to engage in M&As, but they were the most likely to use price restructuring as their strategic move.

Overall, industries tend to exhibit patterns, and we know that executives do too. Use these historical habits to help assess which of the potential moves your competitor will likely select.

As you try to assess which tactics the competitor will choose, remember to think about how quickly they'll be able to move, how large an investment it will require, what the potential risks are of each of the moves, and whether some choices are more likely given historical patterns of behavior. You shouldn't assign specific percentages to each of the potential moves. That creates too much precision that you can't really justify and will only narrow everyone's attention to the move with the largest number attached. Instead, you should rank order the potential competitor strategies along each criterion and see which one rises to the top along the most dimensions. Remember, this is still just guidance. As you gather more information about the competitor while observing their actions, update the expected rankings to see if there is confirmation of your original estimate or whether you need to shift your focus of where they might move.

Final Thoughts

Here's the first piece of overarching advice: don't do this for all your competitors, all the time! This is a selective process. Apply these steps periodically for competitors that have most often surprised you with moves that felt "out of the blue" or for those you feel would have the biggest impact on your operations if they made a strategic shift. Be targeted with the initial list of competitor organizations whose potential moves you track. The framework in this chapter should not take weeks and weeks to put together—you can start with just a brainstorming session among your team to think about all these questions and see where it leads with regard to the initial competitor set. You can then decide for which of those competitors you want to take more time building out a more in-depth profile describing where they might move spontaneously, or whether to add more competitors to the list.

The goal is not to be exhaustive in your search but to mitigate the chances of a major competitor making a "surprise" move that completely catches you off guard. A higher-level assessment of where the competitor might move, and how significant that would be for your company, helps keep your eyes and ears tuned to what your competitors might be doing. Update this exercise quarterly, or more frequently— say, monthly—if your industry moves that fast, to adjust where you need to focus your attention.

The other benefit to being more systematic about undertaking this process is that it can uncover ideas for your organization to explore. Thinking about what your competitor might do, and why it would make sense for them, should raise the question, "Why can't we do that instead?" We'll explore this further in chapter 6 when we discuss Black Hat and war game exercises, but don't ignore the possibility that your competitive brainstorming could uncover interesting ideas for your company to pursue.

As we discussed in chapter 2, there are two classes of competitors that might require a bit more nuance to the advice in this chapter. The first are entrepreneurs. In some sense, thinking about an entrepreneur's strategic moves is the same as what we explored in chapter 2. Entrepreneurs rarely make a major shift in direction while they are initially establishing themselves. They'll adjust and adapt their tactics as they face market pressures, but they'll be unlikely to create another new, innovative product or to enter new geographies and markets before they've established themselves with their first offering. Figuring out the entrepreneur's strategic mindset—as detailed in chapter 2—is sufficient to position yourself so that you aren't surprised by the choices they will make.

It is also critically important for entrepreneurs to consider incumbents' strategic moves. Steve Case has a wonderful quote in his book *The Third Wave*:

> Despite AOL's success, there was always a feeling that just around the corner, there could be a new technology lurking—a fierce new competitor ready to pounce. There were a few startups popping up, and we kept our eyes on them, but most of our fears were focused on the big companies making moves in the space. Some of the world's largest and best-capitalized companies— General Electric, Microsoft, and AT&T among them—were plotting to enter the market, and we worried that if they attacked with overwhelming force, we could be squashed.[8]

The second type of competitor that requires a bit more thought is a privately owned one. In particular, this could be either of the two types we discussed before: private equity–owned and family-owned businesses. The biggest challenge is obtaining financial information on these owners and determining whether they think the time is ripe for a strategic change.

Private equity owners typically make decisions from the same playbook from company to company within a portfolio and from fund to fund. So review whether the specific private equity firm tends to make multiple, periodic strategy adjustments at the companies they own or if they tend to buy a company, install new management to change the overall strategic direction, and then execute on that new plan. If it is the latter, then you don't need to worry as much about a change in strategy midstream. For family-owned businesses, strategic changes often accompany changes in leadership: the next generation takes over and wants to put their own imprint on the company. As long as the company is doing well, and there is no change in leadership, there's less of a concern the family-owned business will spontaneously change its strategy.

Our survey wasn't able to differentiate between private equity–owned and family-owned companies, but we do know if the response came from a public or private (or nonprofit) company. When asked why the business unit changed its strategic direction, private companies were less likely than publicly owned companies to report it was because the strategy was not meeting objectives. Private companies were also less likely to indicate it was because of a change in business unit leadership. However, the privately owned companies were more likely to change direction because the previous strategy had run its course, external changes in the environment led to new opportunities, and new corporate leadership wanted to change the strategic direction.

The survey also shed light on the operational implications of privately owned firms' strategies and tactics. These companies are less likely to use a standard strategic planning process to generate the new strategy (50 percent compared to 57 percent for publicly owned firms). Privately owned companies are more likely to use an ad hoc process because no strategic planning process exists (13 to 8 percent, respectively). You can still assess private companies' historical patterns regarding risk and types of functional moves. For private equity firms, evaluate how they've enacted strategic change at the previous portfolio companies they've owned.

There is disagreement about how many basic story structures exist; estimates range from three[9] to seven[10] to thirty-six.[11] Whatever the correct number is, it is likely that Hollywood studios will continue to simultaneously release movies with the same thematic elements, locations, or characters. The same is true in any industry. There's always a chance a competitor will unexpectedly shift to a new strategy that challenges your organization or throws your plans into chaos. But asking a few questions can provide you with an assessment of whether the competitor might be preparing to make a strategic shift and what that move might be. Following this process will increase the chances you'll be the only one releasing the next blockbuster to the market—not a copycat of your competitor's star attraction.

III Pull Back the Curtain

5 Lessons from Other Professionals

When most people think of archaeological sites, they imagine Pompeii, King Tut's tomb, or *Raiders of the Lost Ark*. Each example is a perfectly preserved site, but rarely do archaeologists find an ancient society in a state as if they were frozen in the middle of everyday life or with a complete collection of what was placed with the deceased when the tomb was sealed. Instead, these historical hunters have to piece together their best explanation for how the society lived and worked as a community from remnants of pottery or figurines, charred remains of food, and piles of buried garbage.

It's not just ancient human societies that researchers have a hard time reconfiguring. *Iguanodon* was one of the first named dinosaurs—it was the second species excavated out of the ground. Despite its early status as a famous, groundbreaking fossil, paleontologists continued to study it, especially as further fossils were found. Scientists later determined that the original *Iguanodon* specimen was actually a combination of four distinct species of dinosaurs. The combination of multiple creatures led the earlier researchers to believe it was a one-hundred-foot-long monster. In addition, the distinctive spike they found with the other bone fossils was assumed to be part of its face (a defensive horn-like appendage), but paleontologists later realized it was actually part of its hand and functioned like an opposable thumb—and dagger for use against predators.

The *Iguanodon* was not the only early dinosaur to undergo further revision as future excavations unearthed more information. *Megalosaurus*, the very first dinosaur unearthed, walked on two legs, but paleontologists originally thought it walked on four legs. This early assumption led them to believe it was a slow-moving plodder, but subsequent research revealed its true bipedal stance and the fact that it was very nimble and quick on its feet.

That's the nature of archaeology and paleontology: new data and new information is always leading to new findings. The incomplete nature of the fossil record and buried remains from ancient civilizations adds to the confusion. That dinosaur skeleton you saw on the recent trip to the natural history museum had some bones that were plaster replicas or were "best guesses" at what the missing bones looked like.

In addition to the challenge of incomplete data and evidence, paleontologists and archaeologists are also confronted by an inability to directly interrogate the subject they are studying. There are no living dinosaurs, and you can't talk with the members of an ancient civilization. They're not alone. The same constraint is true for other professions, including homicide detectives and NICU nurses. NICU nurses talk to newborn babies all the time, but they don't get meaningful responses that tell them the baby's pain on a scale of one to ten. What seems like a meaningful response can often indicate something completely different. Parents assume their newborn smiling means they're happy and connecting with them emotionally. But they're not; the NICU nurses all know it really means the baby has gas.

Competitive insight strategists face the same constraints as these professionals: you cannot talk directly to your competitors and ask them why they made a particular move or how they plan to act in the future. The frameworks we've discussed in the previous chapters have been faced with the same challenges the other professionals confront: incomplete data (on the competitor's business) and an inability to directly interrogate them about their motivations.

I interviewed over two dozen professionals from these four fields and have synthesized their insights into guidance for the business strategist.[1] You don't need to know how to assess whether a newborn has a kidney problem or how to carbon-date charred organic remains from an archaeological excavation. You don't need to understand how to process a crime scene and maintain chain of custody for court appearances. And you certainly don't need to dig through layers of rock to find a shared dinosaur ancestor between a chicken and *T. rex*. But you can understand how these experts approach the analytic and problem-solving challenges they face, how they create a mindset to avoid getting locked into a particular way of thinking, and the tips and tricks they've developed to improve the efficiency of gathering and analyzing the information that is available.

There are ten lessons for competitive insight that emerge from the interviews. Some of them are relevant for how to structure your analyses, like the frameworks in part II. The rest are for structuring your organization, which are the topics of the remaining chapters in part III. I'd like to set the stage by referencing what an archaeologist shared about one of the core challenges in their field: "You can't get into ancient peoples' heads." You know what they did (based on the evidential remnants we find), which is influenced by what they were thinking, but we can never know for certain their thought processes and motivations. This is also the fundamental challenge about competitors: we can never truly know what's going on in their head. But by observing what they've done (based on the evidence in the market), which is influenced by what they were trying to do, we can try to predict what they might do in the future.

Lesson 1: Build a Diverse Team

One of the strongest results from the interviews was the recommendation by virtually all of the interviewees to surround yourself with a diverse team. Much has been written recently about the importance of diversity, equity, and inclusion in the workplace, and deservedly so. What was so striking was this result wasn't the purpose of the study. I was not seeking to make a diversity argument with the questions asked, but it comes forth nonetheless. In particular, building a team of people with different backgrounds, experiences, and expertise was important to surface additional key information.

Paleontology seems like it mostly deals with digging fossils out of the ground, but the field has expanded to include specialists in other fields who've chosen to focus on the application of their skills to life forms that used to live on Earth. Examples include paleochemists, physicists, geochemists, geologists, mathematicians, and architects. Physicists help analyze how the force of impact from walking affects the structure and density of leg bones, while architects help build models of dinosaurs. Chemistry helped solve a fossil record riddle of the color of dinosaur eggs. In the modern world, birds are the only animals that have colored eggs (although not all bird eggs are colored). Since birds and dinosaurs had a common ancestor, it's natural to wonder whether at least some of their eggs were similarly colored. Unfortunately, when eggs fossilize, they don't preserve their coloration. But there is a chemical residue in colored bird eggs, so working with a paleochemist, a team of paleontologists found the same chemical residue in the fossilized dinosaur eggs. Digging up fossils alone would not have solved the riddle.

NICU nurses also benefit from diverse voices in the team. Everyone who is caring for the newborn has different specialties and scan for different things in the patient record. Sitting together or walking on rounds as a group, the team presents each baby's status, which raises different concerns. No idea is stupid, which leads to a supportive environment and group dialogue. NICUs also have care coordinators managing a few babies at a time to ensure consistent messaging with the parents and across the team. The NICU nurses talk with other providers (e.g., doctors, nurses, pharmacists, nutritionists) within their hospital and sometimes even reach out to colleagues in different cities to get advice, for example, on the safety and efficacy of COVID vaccinations for pregnant women.

Archaeology teams can number up to fifteen to twenty specialists. These include team members with local language skills (and local advocates who can help with securing excavation rights and local community buy-in) and expertise in soil, pottery, chemistry, metallurgy, animal remains, botanical remains, and figurines among others. Their networks are broad in scope as the researchers talk with teams on other sites—locally and internationally, wherever the relevant expertise exists—and the networks are constantly evolving since excavation site needs change. This broad expertise is essential for extracting useful information as quickly as possible, which is critical given the limited time for excavating on-site. Your question might not be answered by you, but someone else—somewhere—may be able to answer it. There's a reason academic papers in the discipline can have upward of a dozen authors: they each offer a different point of view and unique contribution to the overall conclusion.

Take, for example, an archaeologist who studies figurines. The archaeologist was researching an example crafted from antlers, which was unusual since they are typically made from clay or bone. The shape was clear, but its use was open to reasonable speculation. They were uncertain what to make of antler as the material, so they read up on deer hunting and talked with hunters back home. One mentioned that antlers are hot to touch because of the blood flow in them, which the researcher hadn't known. Some cultures ascribe a magical quality to them as a result. That insight helped provide crucial clues to the reason for the antler's use as a material.

Another diversity dimension is how some archaeologists take a micro view, while others take a macro one. Those with micro views focus on pottery from a single site, exploring the specifics of the clay, paint, and design. Those with macro views scan fifteen sites within a region to seek patterns and larger connections across the locations. Both of these views are valuable for putting together a picture of the culture.

Several archaeologists (and paleontologists) mentioned the value of graduate students on the team. While there was acknowledgment of certain university requirements to provide graduate students with training, there was also the understanding that they come with a different perspective, in particular being more in touch with the leading technologies. Their inexperience in the field also allows them to see and interpret things with a fresh perspective.

Finally, archaeological sites exist all over the world, and the people that created them years ago did not all have the same worldview. For example, Western societies have different mindsets than Native American and First Nation tribes, where rocks, trees, and wind have spirits and need to be treated with respect. There is an inherent bias that can come into play when Western-educated researchers try to explain other cultures from their own viewpoint. Instead, they need to view the culture and site from the mindset of the society at the time.

As a competitive analyst, look for a coherent answer between all the perspectives on your team. Include strategists, supply chain experts, marketers, and individuals with different cultural backgrounds and of different genders to provide you with a broad set of perspectives. As an archaeologist shared, knowing there has to be a coherent answer among all the perspectives helps—there must be something that ties everything together to explain all the different pieces the previous society left behind. There was a physical event in the past that everyone can put their unique perspective on, and that physical event must have been a product of all the different inputs from the individuals living in that culture. Use your diverse team to triangulate on the common explanation for why the competitor is behaving the way they are.

Lesson 2: Know the Question You're Trying to Answer

There are two schools of thought for how to logically approach a problem. One says to be inductive: gather lots of data and figure out the best explanation that best fits all the pieces. The second is to be deductive: craft a theory to explain what you think is the right answer and then gather data to test whether your hypothesis is correct. This is a challenge with all types of problem solving, including trying to predict your competitor. Should you gather a multitude of facts about the competitor and see which story falls into place to explain their pricing behavior (inductive)? Or should you start with a hypothesis of why your competitor prices their products a certain way and then gather data to prove or disprove it (deductive)? In both cases, you have to know you're trying to determine the pricing behavior (and not the innovation or partnership strategy), but how you approach answering the question differs. If you are hoping that I will tell you the "correct" answer, then I'm sorry to disappoint. However, I would like to share some insights from the other professionals that provide guidance.

In general, those I spoke with admitted there is tension in their fields on whether it's best to form a hypothesis and test it or to let the data guide you to the right conclusion even if it doesn't fit any preconceived hypotheses. While most fell on the side of starting with a hypothesis, many said that what ultimately ends up occurring is that you move back and forth between inductive and deductive reasoning. Start with a hypothesis and then collect data. If it supports your hypothesis, keep digging for more data, and if it doesn't, then instead of starting over, mine that data for insights that help craft the next hypothesis. Go collect more data and continue to iterate. The key, though, is that you always must have a question in mind. You always need to have a target you are working to explain. Even when you are out collecting data, it should be purposeful and not random. It should help you lead to some question of interest.

One archaeologist framed the challenge as asking small and large questions. This is similar to the micro and macro views discussed previously. For example, why do skulls get decapitated and left in a cave? Why paint on cave walls and hide the images deep within the cave's recesses? These are smaller questions that can help understand choices of individuals or part of the culture's story. Big questions, on the other hand, are more systemic: Why does a culture transition from hunter/gatherer to settled? Do cultures transition because of climate shifts or population growth? Why did Greek colonizers move to Italy? Earliest cave paintings are all animals and very few humans—why? Where are all the people?

Some researchers prefer to address the small questions and some like tackling the big questions. Others bridge the two by tacking back and forth between studying small questions to build inferences about the big questions of interest and then going back to small questions to support the big picture answers. (Some don't go back and forth, though—they find what they're good at and stick with it.) Paleontologists also focus on different dimensions. Some tackle small questions, such as what the dinosaurs at a particular site ate or if they worked in a pack. Others tackle large questions, like what drove the evolution of feathers on dinosaurs. Neither is better than the other; they are mutually required to arrive at the ultimate explanation.

The sequential nature of forming theories, finding data, and then updating the theories based on that information was raised repeatedly in the interviews. Archaeologists need to constantly reevaluate assumptions, often on a daily, or sometimes hourly, basis. As you dig down, you uncover new insights of how material was deposited on top of the previous layers. The further you dig, the more you might have to change your plans. It's like having a conversation with the site: you are excavating and collecting data and listening to what the evidence is telling you, and then you ask new questions and reorient and recalibrate your plans. It can drive students on the dig nuts because yesterday the implication was one thing based on their findings, and the next day they find something different, and now there's an entirely new hypothesis!

On one dig site, the ground-penetrating radar wasn't finding anything of real interest, but there was a signature of something that wasn't clear and didn't look like anything found before. It wasn't very big, so it didn't initially seem interesting, but the team dug it out and realized it was a stone step. This was significant because it helped them identify where the buildings were located. The next time they saw this radar image, they knew it wasn't an insignificant anomaly but was likely to be another stone step.

Archaeologists do background research before digging. The more they know about the site, the less time they need to spend excavating, which is the expensive part of the research. They also talk with people on the ground in the location of interest, including nonarchaeologists and those who are avocationally or nonprofessionally interested in the field. The archaeologists ask what those others have found in the area and what stories they've heard from people living there. Reading widely helps too—both within the field and outside of archaeological literature—to challenge assumptions. While reading about the downfall of General Electric, one archaeologist framed the lessons on conglomerates, organizational structure, management culture, and managers in terms of the implications for understanding the downfall of ancient societies. As another archaeologist put it, think outside the trench.

For the business strategist, the takeaway is you must have a clear question about your competitor that you are trying to answer. Is it a question you can address, such as what is the impact of their social media campaign on their future product portfolio shifts? Or is it one that is much harder to assess, such as what is the impact of their personnel policies on employee satisfaction? As you collect more data, update the questions you ask—say, shifting to how their influencer connections could lead to new beauty care products in Europe. As you prove or disprove hypotheses, update your beliefs about the competitor as discussed in chapter 1.

Lesson 3: Be Systematic When Collecting Data

Competitive strategists should be collecting lots of information on their competitors from many different sources, both within and outside of the organization. It's a challenge to get the appropriate data to understand competitors, but it's also hard to put your hands on the right data at the right time to create actionable insights. Competitive insight analysts often don't have the luxury of being able to interrogate the information sources again, so the data needs to be collected accurately and comprehensively from the start. Luckily, this is a process the experts I spoke with have spent years addressing (if not perfecting).

Rule number one is to have a process to follow and to document everything excessively and thoroughly. As the detective I spoke with said, unorganized cases don't get solved.

Paleontologists collect immense amounts of data when they're "in the field." They don't have to analyze all of it initially, but they like having it in case they need to answer those questions in the future. It's very hard to return and capture data again, so if you're there and it's available, you should get it. You never know what data you will need tomorrow when you collect today. To help with that, have a detailed list of what you plan to collect so you don't get distracted when you're in the field. This has the added benefit of freeing up your mind to explore tangents without getting lost down the rabbit hole.

The paleontologists also recommend having an eye for details and not letting anything escape as being "too small" to matter. Not every fossil is the size of a *Titanosaurus* femur, but every fragment that survives is a potential piece of the puzzle. (I was fortunate to spend a day on a dig site, and I spent the first thirty minutes collecting fossilized bone fragments that had washed downhill from an exposed *Triceratops* squamosal.) Cast a wide net and collect more evidence since you won't find one magical piece of proof. The gradual accumulation of data leads to the significant findings. One fossil doesn't mean much on its own, while ten can still lead to large randomness across outcomes. But having hundreds of pieces of corroborating evidence can identify the small variations that make a difference. This requires patience, even in the field. Keep your eye on the landscape as you walk. Stop and look around, letting your eye fall on seemingly random things. If you rush, you might walk right past a significant finding.

Another challenge with finding the right data is the need to find a place where others haven't looked yet. The K–Pg boundary is the layer of Earth with a high concentration of iridium. This is the layer above which there are no dinosaur fossils and below which they are found. Hence, it is the marker for when the meteorite killed off the dinosaurs (meteorites have an abundance of iridium). Knowing this, paleontologists tend to overcollect near the K–Pg boundary. This oversampling biases the results of what is "typical" of dinosaur existence. Fossilization occurs across time, and species turn over throughout time, and the sampling regime should be distributed across that range of lifetimes.

It's standard practice in archaeology to document, document, document, with the use of photos and drawings. This is especially helpful for being able to make connections to other archaeologists' future findings. One found an abundance of blue-colored material, but even though they didn't know what the remnants represented, the blue pieces were separated and placed in a bag for storage. A few years later, when reading about another find of blue egg shells used for head dresses at a different site, they were able to go back to their bag and reexamine the blue pieces in a new light. They didn't have to recreate that data; it was already categorized and ready for analysis.

Archaeologists optimize their time spent digging by exploring the surface of the site first. The better picture they can create from topography, remnants on the surface, ground-penetrating radar images, histories of the peoples who have lived in the area, and so on, the more efficient they will be when excavating. Much like a doctor diagnoses the patient before cutting them open for surgery, archaeologists diagram the expected findings as best as possible before putting shovel to dirt.

Archaeologists can't save everything that's excavated, and often times the objects can't leave the host country. One interviewee reported that colleagues had found numerous figurines at a site in Greece, but they couldn't be taken outside of the country. Photos were taken to document where and how they were found, but the archaeologists also secured a 3D printer to make replicas to take home. The tactile experience of holding the copy allowed for a deeper understanding than the 2D photos and drawings could. Of course, that was in addition to all the standard measurements, photos, drawings, Munsell soil color chart comparisons (to assess the color of clay objects), Mohs hardness kit scratch tests of the materials to assess compositions, maps of the horizontal (things on the same level) and vertical (at different depths) dimensions, and so forth. All of the data can be put into a database to analyze thousands of pieces across multiple sites to find connections that would not be possible otherwise (such as the percentage of clay that was locally sourced for the objects).

To many, archaeology seems like a big, bold field—Indiana Jones finding the treasure in the jungle. But as we've seen, the detailed analysis of individual artifacts and portions of a site is the bulk of the work. Sometimes, the data is not evident to the naked eye and needs to be revealed through microscopic analysis. For example, the presence of certain isotopes in the remnants can indicate what the civilization was eating. On the other hand, sometimes stepping back and seeing the big, macro views can provide insight, oftentimes built upon the accumulation of the smaller details. (Recall from lesson 2 that archaeologists either specialize in micro or macro analysis, or they vacillate between them.) One archaeologist was able to identify a buried city on the top of a mountain because of a longer-term project to explore the Silk Road. If a site existed, it should have been on the Silk Road path previously uncovered and documented, which ran near the mountain top. A surface scan subsequently confirmed there was something underneath the ground, and the team successfully excavated the site. Sometimes all the data is already there—you just need it organized in such a way that you can draw out the necessary insights.

The NICU nurses also shared that everything has to be documented for each baby—from head to toe—each day and shared across shifts. One of the NICU nurses shared the process in our discussion, and it took ten to fifteen minutes to cover everything. If they don't follow the same procedure for each baby, things get missed. It helps them catch things down the line as even subtle changes occur (for preemie babies, small changes are relatively big in comparison to adults). The process puts them in the mindset for analyzing the newborn's condition. If they get interrupted, it is hard to go back and pick up without referring to the process.

One caveat shared by a nurse was that sometimes you *don't* want to collect all potential data—in their case by deciding *not* to perform a certain test. If the fetus in the mother has an abnormal brain scan, say, at thirty-two weeks, then they could use the MRI machine to figure out why. But if it doesn't change anything in the next eight weeks or upon delivery, it would be better to wait until after delivery to perform the scan. There are always test you could do. Families always want answers right now, and the inclination is to help provide those answers. But sometimes it's a better use of resources to wait to collect superior data that will provide more insight.

This is a valuable lesson for the business strategist who is being pressured to assess a competitor. Others in the organization want to know *right now* what the competitor is doing, often because the organization itself is planning to make a strategic move. But sometimes you need to hold off and get a better answer in a couple of weeks when more data is available, especially if the answer is not time critical. And even if the answer is time critical, you might be better off making a prediction based on the information at hand and then updating in the future once new information is revealed (e.g., the competitor releases their quarterly earnings report). It is sometimes as valuable to decide what *not* to do when formulating strategy, and the same can apply to competitive insight.[2]

A key piece of advice from the detective deals with how to extract data from individuals who can talk (e.g., the witness and background character interviews): don't ask leading questions. Open-ended questions allow the other person to fill in the blanks, and you learn things you never would have otherwise. Silence can be valuable too: ask the question and let the other person fill in the words. The more time you provide, the more they will fill it with important information.

In business, we have the luxury of being able to go back to customers and suppliers to confirm information. We can call up colleagues in other divisions to learn what they know. But we can't do that with competitors. Additionally, others in your organization are likely not documenting their knowledge of competitors as the information is often composed of thoughts and impressions off the top of their heads. The competitive insight function (see chapter 7) must systematically collect and organize the knowledge so it's available to anyone when it's needed for a strategic decision.

Lesson 4: Measure Things Correctly

A corollary challenge to systemically collecting data is the issue of whether you are measuring things correctly. Mismeasurement can provide you with the wrong conclusions about your competitor, which makes the data collection effort irrelevant.

The NICU nurses shared how they use the metric system to measure the preemies' length and weight as well as the measurements for medicine dosages. This is done even in the United States, where the metric system is not widely used because it is more specific. Remember, these are really small babies, so differences in a millimeter can matter. Precision and detail are critical because there is not a large margin for error. The prepackaged kits with medical instruments come in a range of sizes covering birth weights from 500 g (about 1 pound) up to 5 kg (about 11 pounds); it is not a one-size-fits-all endeavor.

The rate of fossilization in the Earth's crust is not uniform. In particular, there are gaps between the "last" dinosaur fossils in the ground and the K–Pg boundary—with a perfect record, there should be fossils right at the boundary. They are not always there, which means time passed between the last fossil being created and the end of the dinosaurs. That doesn't mean the meteorite *wasn't* the cause of their demise (that's still the consensus) but that we don't have perfect visibility into what happened in the final year they were on Earth. As you dig deeper, the gap between the current fossil and the next one down in the earth may be one thousand years. Those gaps in the data are not dissimilar to the gaps in available data on competitors—you need to adjust your insights for the time between observations to get a true picture (e.g., the pace of failed innovation attempts at the competitor since you can often only see the "wins" that make it to market).

Trust data quality over quantity. Business leaders have had "big data" ingrained as a mantra, but bigger is not always better. One paleontologist said certain databases are unreliable even though there is a lot of data, and thus they don't provide better insights. Use data of better quality even if it is less abundant. You should ideally collect your own data instead of solely relying on predeveloped, third-party databases.

One important area of focus in archaeology is metrology, the study of measurement. Ancient peoples didn't use standard units of linear measurement, so the foot measure was different across cities (e.g.,

Athens versus Sparta). Weights were standardized because of their basis for creating value in coins minted in different locations but not linear unit measurements. This creates a problem for assessing the correct unit of measurement at a particular site. It requires reverse engineering and looking for patterns across buildings or sites in an area, but once you find the pattern, the design falls into place.

One of the archaeologists tried to determine the design scheme for a council house by working with different diameter circles, eventually finding a size that fit the inside dimension. From wall to wall, six blocks of sixteen feet each, or ninety-six feet long, fit exactly. Subsequent measurements yielded a one-hundred-foot-long building when including the wall thickness. Since one hundred feet was a sacred unit of measurement, this implied a one-hundred-foot temple or sacred building. Understanding the basic design and geometry and how the structure is laid out on the ground requires figuring out what units of measurement that designer used. Doing that helps get one closest to the mind of the designer—how this person with basic geometric forms and dimensions put together a scheme that could be communicated to others and built in the community.

One final piece of advice about measurement from the archaeologists is to vary the way in which you measure things to take in different vantage points. A regional survey of the land and environment and collection of villages provides a systemic view of how multiple locations interacted with each other. More detailed excavation on each particular site will uncover specific activities at that individual city. This is the difference between corporate strategy and scope analysis of the competitor (across all their divisions) versus business unit analysis (for a particular product category in a particular geography)—recall our discussion of corporate scope in chapter 2. And similar to archaeologists also thinking about digging horizontally (house to house at a particular layer) versus vertically (pits that show how layers of the civilization were deposited over time), business strategists must consider competitors from horizontal (across a set of divisions) and vertical (along a particular value chain) dimensions. Both are important but for answering different questions.

Lesson 5: Plan Explicitly What to Do with the Data

It's important to collect the data and get the measurements correct, but you also need to have a plan for what to do with the data once you have it. This is connected to lesson 2: know the question you're trying to answer.

The NICU nurses spoke of having a consistent objective every day for all the babies: an eventual, safe discharge home. Nurses use algorithms to determine whether the baby is gaining weight and eating sufficiently in order to go home. And there is a separate algorithm they use when there is an emergency, represented by ABC: airway, breathing, circulation. The use of these algorithms provides a consistent method in which to analyze the data they collect. One newborn had been through a rough delivery, which sometimes can cause fluid in the lungs. After being in the NICU for a few days, the baby seemed to have recovered enough to be discharged. But that day, their oxygen levels kept dropping and then returning to normal. Since this was a new symptom, the baby couldn't go home.

They then put the baby on a machine from a different company, but the oxygen levels were still dropping. They went through a checklist of possibilities: Poor neurological development? Pneumonia? Fluid in lungs? Collapsed lung? Abnormality in lungs? Airway blocked? Everything looked normal. They moved on to checking the heart next. The EKG looked fine, so they did an echocardiogram (to test the blood flow in the heart chambers), which uncovered a heart defect: a hole between the aorta and the heart that was causing fresh and used blood to mix. The hole was subsequently fixed and the baby was able to go home, but without the structured process for diagnosing the problem, it may have taken them much longer to find the solution.

One paleontologist shared they always write down what they're going to do when they get home from the dig site because they assume they'll forget everything on the long trek home. What was the order we were going to look at the fossils? What were we going to compare them to? Who else was I going to contact for input? There are so many things you can do with the data that it's easy to forget the plan if it's not written down. For one study, they were searching for micro teeth in samples of soil they had collected. They used a standard process: take one cubic centimeter (cc) of soil and search it for teeth. Do that for a minimum of five batches. If you find at least five micro teeth, then you've got a hit and you continue adding one cc at a time. But if those first five cc don't yield anything, move on to another sample. Without a definitive rubric, the team could get lost sifting through everything.

Another paleontologist shared that they focus on the data and initial findings that signify big orders of magnitude changes. If there is a significantly large change indicated, it's either really important or a mistake. Either way, be sure you can explain that anomaly before delving into the data or else it will be harder to draw conclusions.

One archaeologist said that they focus on questions to falsify certain hypotheses. For example, was a site an economic or religious center? It's hard to positively prove which one is correct, but if you can organize your data to show it couldn't have been used as an economic center, then you have narrowed the potential set of explanations. If you have more confidence in knowing what you don't know, then you can use that to set up where to look for falsification. For example, there is no naturally occurring stone near Poverty Point in Louisiana, so all stone used at the site had to have been imported. How far it came, and what it was used for, provide clues about the value the society placed on obtaining that stone material. If the stone was not used in any of the other spiritual locations at the site, then that doesn't prove it was an economic center, but it would increase confidence that it was not primarily a religious center.

The final warning from the archaeologists relates to the documentary evidence, or texts that were written at the time of the society being studied. It had been assumed that these written records were the correct answer for what was happening at the time and the related motivations. However, archaeological study sometimes tells a different story from those texts, partially because the written records were often created by the civilization's "winners" and only rarely by those without power. You should definitely pay attention to what your competitor is saying—read their press releases—but as highlighted in chapter 1, you should take their statements with a grain of salt. Compare what they say with the assets and resources they can use in addition to what you know about the individual decision maker.

As you build competitive insight, be sure you have a coherent plan for how the data collected will be used to analyze the competitor. Start with simple assumptions about the competitor and only add complication as needed, especially because the more complex the analysis, the harder it will be to find data and solutions and the harder it will be to communicate your insights to the rest of your organization.

Lesson 6: Seek Patterns

The ability to find and use analogies is a skill every business strategist should have in their toolkit. These can be examples of other companies' strategic moves in previous time periods, in different geographies, or in other industries. Being able to apply these analogies to the context in which you operate can provide you with a wealth of new ideas. To be successful, you need to be able to select the right parallels and similarities. The interviewees—especially the paleontologists and archaeologists—shared how seeking patterns was crucial.

Archaeology and paleontology are historical sciences, meaning you can't run experiments (just like you can't experiment on your competitors). You often first need to start with a hypothesis of what is similar to your situation, such as modern analogies to dinosaurs. One challenge with analogies, and assessing what is similar, is the fact that human imagination can be limited. Pterosaurs—winged animals that looked like flying dinosaurs but weren't dinos—have no modern equivalent. But they are sort of like a cross between a bird and a crocodile, which are the closest living descendants to dinosaurs. Are there other living animals—especially among the ten thousand extant birds—that are most similar?

Spinosaurus was the only aquatic dinosaur (we know about), which raises the interesting question of why others weren't also aquatic, or at least semiaquatic (like amphibians). One paleontologist studied the bone density of numerous extant vertebrates and found that aquatic creatures have denser bones. This prevents them from becoming so buoyant that they can't swim down to chase prey. The paleontologist moved on to look at sections of dinosaur bones and found their bone density pattern matches that of current land animals. *Spinosaurus's* bone density, on the other hand, was like that of a whale or a penguin. The pattern of bone density across living vertebrates and dinosaurs helped explain why *Spinosaurus* was a uniquely aquatic dinosaur.

Evolution is a series of historical patterns, so paleontologists seek analogous situations, collect data from the ancient time period of interest, and see if it fits the pattern. If not, they get more data and find another analogous comparison to see if that pattern fits better. You can even seek analogies from other fields (like business leaders should from other industries or geographies). One paleontologist compared the decline in stock volatility (those with high beta values tend to go bankrupt or become "extinct") to the decline in volatility of genera and families (species origination and extinction declines over time). The similar pattern across the two was driven by different factors, but the underlying consistency implies there could be more universal constraints on evolution. That same paleontologist compared the decline of species to the decline of technologies like the steam engine as it was supplanted by more effective means.

One researcher shared their work on the earliest ancestors of monkeys. For a long time, these were thought to have originated in Africa since that's where apes and humans evolved. However, the paleontologist found fossils in Asia that were older and more primitive than those found in Africa, so primitive that it wasn't clear if they were monkey ancestors at all. When the Asian monkey ancestor fossils were first found, they were very tiny and didn't appear as expected. But when compared to textbook fossil drawings of primate evolutionary history, they matched. Over the next ten to fifteen years, more fossils were found in Asia that were older and smaller than any found in Africa. If monkeys originated in Asia, how did they arrive in Africa, which was an island at the time?

Similar fossils were subsequently found in Libya—so similar it was as if the Libyan fossils were from the first monkeys that had swum from Asia to Africa. In fact, the teeth explained the story since mammal teeth are like crime scene fingerprints; you can identify a species with only one tooth in the jaw. The Libyan monkey teeth were so close to teeth of Asian fossils that they appeared to be the same species in the same location. Either they had independently evolved in two separate places (a conjecture paleontologists don't like) or the Asian monkeys migrated to Africa.

Ignoring history can lead to errors of association. *Archaeopteryx* was a bird-like dinosaur, but it had biogenetically branched off the tree of life before the common bird ancestor had evolved. Many specimens of *Archaeopteryx* in many different sizes have been found, and it was assumed they were many different species because each had a fully feathered tail. Modern birds don't grow tail feathers until after they leave the nest; since *Archaeopteryx* tails were full feathered, it was assumed they must all be adults, just like birds. The different sizes must mean there were different species of varying dimensions. But the mistake is the parallel with the birds since *Archaeopteryx* evolved separately from birds. The juveniles of the *Archaeopteryx* ancestors were also fully feathered (including the tails), so it is merely a trait of that genus. Applying modern bird traits to *Archaeopteryx* without thinking about the historical order of events results in a faulty analogy.

Archaeologists also seek patterns to explain ancient civilizations. Some principles are foundational, such as those used to find where nomadic settlements had been: water nearby, shade, near mountains, and so on. Using these patterns narrows the field of potential sites to search. Other questions have a range of potential patterns that could fit. For example, the household-level insight may not mesh with those derived from the entire site or a set of sites in the region. In terms of behavior, there's a tendency to fall into assuming there was either a zero-sum game competition between individuals or that they acted for the good of the whole community. Many times, however, the true answer lies in the gray area between. In addition, the pattern can change over time regarding where it falls in the range (e.g., shifting from individual focus to group focus and then back).

Archaeologists are exposed to many different ways of forming a society. They have an expansive library for ways a group of people can organize. When there is an unknown observation for a civilization being studied, they search to find the closest resemblance from that library. There may be nothing since the ethnographic record is limited (more has been lost to time about human societal organization than there is evidence of what we do today), so they have to be open to alternative explanations and multiple societal structures. This is no different from how businesses can organize themselves in a myriad of ways across industries and geographies and time, which is your library compendium as a competitive strategist.

Context matters: if only one instance of behavior is found, it's hard to figure out an explanation, but multiple recurring instances begins to lead to a pattern. Archaeologists compare from site to site even if they only dig in one place. They talk with others and leverage their experience on other digs, and they seek out examples from other fields or time periods. Sometimes these go far afield. One archaeologist shared that when trying to understand the networks between nomadic populations, they sought out research on how internet gamers form their connections. The modern digital age can provide clues to civilizations in ancient Roman times!

One archaeologist used business analogies to understand a set of figurines. Sometimes just the clay legs remained, and other times only a single leg was left. The single legs appeared to have been purposely split or snapped apart. The researcher speculated that these "split legs" represented pieces from a rudimentary contract (like a bond coupon in preelectronic days). While the figurines could have served religious purposes, the archaeologist suggested they were more likely used for trading and keeping track of some kind of transaction.

As you search for patterns, you still need to be sensitive to outliers. Another archaeologist told of finding pottery and tools from the period of interest on a site's surface, but they also found remnants from a much earlier time period, which seemed rather odd. Since they were searching for a more recent find, and the site looked like a recent site, they assumed the old tools were an anomaly. Seven years later, a colleague joined the excavation who was a skilled archaeologist, just not in that particular location or time period. Because the new researcher had a certain level of ignorance about what to expect, they were open to viewing the anomalies as the key to understanding the site. It turned out the site contained the oldest mounds in the Americas. The original archaeologist knew what they were seeing—they recognized them as early pottery and tools—but chose to ignore them because they were seen as outliers of no value.

When you see a pattern and lock it in, when you can explain all the patterns and they fit together, it feels euphoric—like you cracked a secret code. But don't rest on your laurels. Spend the rest of the week trying to knock down the idea because others will definitely try to. If your conclusions can survive your own attack, they will likely survive others trying to poke holes in your theory. In the end, you can never be 100 percent sure. "Possibly" is a word often used in archaeology literature. It is the result of answers prone to equifinality: there are two plausible explanations. For example, a site might have been used as an economic and ceremonial center. These are difficult to deal with, so archaeologists try to design experiments as reductively binary as possible so that the answer can't be both possible solutions. If that doesn't work, then find a different method, approach, or site. In the end, there are some times when they still can't decide the correct explanation—in that case, future research is required.

I'll share one final piece of advice from the NICU nurses, who use patterning to compare current cases with previous newborns they had treated. They build up their set of reference cases by running simulations. A physician will enter the NICU with a baby doll and place it down, providing information on the condition of the baby. The nurses have to stop what they're doing to care for the doll—no matter what they were doing. This exercise helps build the capability to shift gears when an emergency arises in addition to allowing the nurses to practice situations they might not have faced with an actual newborn. It's also a good team-building exercise. As we'll see in chapter 6, these simulation techniques are a great way of helping competitive strategists hone their craft.

Analogies and patterns exist throughout the business landscape. We sometimes get caught looking within our own organization or within our own area of responsibility. Let's face it—life is busy and we don't have much free time to explore. But if you want to understand your competitor's mindset, you need to build your own library of analogies and develop pattern-spotting skills.

Lesson 7: Take Advantage of Advances in Technology

Technology is always creating new opportunities for businesses. Big data mining provides customer insights. The digitalization of supply chain interactions allows for greater efficiencies. Even employee satisfaction metrics and profiles can help improve retention and engagement. But, as mentioned in chapter 1, an area where companies haven't invested sufficiently in the latest technology is competitive intelligence. The interviews highlighted just how important technological advances have been to these disciplines—especially the "ancient" ones of paleontology and archaeology—and should encourage a concerted effort to seek technological solutions for developing competitive insight.

Technological advances used by archaeologists in the field are not new to the world or developed exclusively for the profession, but they can be used to improve the survey analysis on, and under, the surface. In prior decades, archaeologists would use laser survey instruments to map sites. It could take days—and usually weeks—to collect the thousands of measurements to finish mapping a site. Today, they use LIDAR— light detection and ranging equipment using laser beams to create a 3D representation of the environment—which takes an afternoon to accomplish the same task. They are also increasingly using airplane (or drone) mapping through GIS platforms. Other techniques borrow from geological and oil exploration for subsurface inspection, like magnetometry, bore holes, and ground-penetrating radar. And MRI machines allow researchers to look inside sealed jars, sarcophagi, or other objects without damaging them. These automated systems are not a panacea, but they can go a long way to being more efficient with the time in the field.

Another tip was to tailor the questions to the technology you can use. Since archaeology is an accretional knowledge, one option is to return to older material and ideas but with the use of new technology. Relying on previously collected data can be problematic because the data wasn't always gathered in ways that are usable by the newer technology. You may have to collect new data, but newer technology could allow you to collect superior data, so it's not all bad news. One interviewee had developed a model in 2001 to analyze how nomadic tribes worked together, thereby defining where trading routes existed, but computing power could not process it sufficiently. So they shelved the data and model and brought it back when technology had evolved fifteen years later—ultimately resulting in a published article. If you reach a dead end because of technology or data, tuck it away to revisit later (e.g., when ML allows for more realistic competitor modeling).

This is admittedly harder to do with competitor data because of the need to create insights immediately, but if you develop a method to assess the competitor's intent and don't have the technological capability to execute the idea, don't discard it. Save those ideas and return to them in the future. Take to heart the advice of one of the archaeologists, who does a two-day workshop on a new technology and then adds an expert on that technology to the team (recall lesson 1). The workshop allows the archaeologist to know the basics so they can better engage with the expert and understand the possibilities for the technology. Knowing the principles creates better collaboration. You don't have to be an expert in everything, but strive to be a jack of all trades conversant in multiple areas: photography, surveying, drawing, and so on for the archaeologist; and marketing, operations, finance, and HR processes for the business strategist.

NICU nurses also use the latest technology to help the newborns under their care. Ultrasound technology is commonly used and keeps improving, and there are many monitoring machines hooked up to babies. As good as the machines are, however, there are many variables that cannot be controlled, such as the mother's stress levels and genetic influences. There is always room for error even though the expectation is 100 percent accuracy. (This isn't that different from the expectation when predicting competitors.) The improved technology helps the nurses be more accurate, though, and strategists should seek technology to improve their predictive ability.

Another NICU nurse said the digitization of health charts saves a lot of time. The information wasn't different from what had been stored on paper charts, but they now have the benefit of being able to quickly compare two charts side by side. They can also explore how data from the same assessment changes over time without having to pull multiple pages from the record. The three-ring binders that used to store preemie charts would be two or three inches thick. Now, all the data is immediately available and searchable, which saves a lot of time and prevents mistakes. Competitive strategists should be inspired to create dashboards to help track their competitors (see chapter 7).

One significant technological change benefiting paleontologists has allowed a fundamental reimagining of the tree of life, or how evolution occurred. Back in the day, evolution trees adhered to the stratophenetics principle. Animals evolved over time, so older fossils were the ancestors, and you connected the dots down the tree to the more recent creatures. It was not necessarily rigorous and prevented paleontologists from locally interpreting the tree as they zoomed in on smaller areas of it. The newer method—cladistics—organizes life forms on the tree based on common characteristics not found in an ancestral group. It seeks the most parsimonious method to create patterns between life forms. The method is only feasible because of computer algorithms creating the simplest possible tree from all the available data, with the fewest convergent lines and no devaluing (a reversal, or evolution of simpler features).

While many different technologies are available to companies, and more developed every year, competitive insight analysts should explore how those technologies can help them better predict their competitors. From text mining software of competitor announcements to social media trackers of the likes, dislikes, and comments about the competition, competitive insight should be as much at the forefront of leveraging technology as the rest of the organization.

Lesson 8: Avoid Getting Locked into One Way of Viewing the World

One of the biggest challenges of any decision-making process is the confirmation bias risk—we start to narrow in on a pet explanation and frame all the data we collect (and how we collect it) to support that hypothesis. This can be especially challenging with trying to understand competitors. We cannot obtain primary source information from competitors to directly contradict our ideas and force us to confront a different answer. We've discussed already how there is uncertainty surrounding the fields of the four professionals, so I asked them how they try to avoid locking onto a particular answer.

First of all, be comforted by the fact most of the interviewees acknowledged this is a big challenge and one they cannot always overcome. The detective shared that all cases are different, so you go where the evidence and witness statements lead. You may follow some branches down a chosen path, but you always have to go back up to the top-level question of who committed the crime and why. They also rely on teamwork. As a homicide officer in charge of a unit, they saw their job as always asking questions and playing the devil's advocate to pressure test the conclusions of the case officers. What else is missing? What else can you do? They have to cover all the bases if they expect to succeed at trial, so the outsider view can help stress test if the current status of the case is as locked up as possible.

Paleontologists also mentioned being a devil's advocate on a team as a valuable support. Pay attention to colleagues with a different mind structure and way of thinking. Ask for their opinion and listen to those critiques. If you have an idea, go discuss it with someone down the hall. If they say you are an idiot, you're not necessarily wrong, but you do need to rethink your analysis and idea. One benefit of academia is that the peer review process automatically creates criticism of any submitted draft. Someone will almost certainly identify problems (the mindset of reviewers is to find fault). As a strategist, seek out others who will push back. You may not feel comfortable doing this, but avoid defaulting to close collaborators because it feels safer (they could be biased in your favor). Cultivate a network of critics; the more you have identified, the greater chance they'll be available when needed. Seek out those who won't be afraid to provide constructive criticism.

Another trick is to continue collecting data even if you think you have the answer. One benefit is that the interpretation will change naturally as more evidence builds up. *Jeholornis* was an early bird-like dinosaur, and for a long time, paleontologists thought a particular chest bone was a lateral trabecula attached to the sternum (these bones help flying creatures with their wing downstroke). But they couldn't figure out how it fit into the sternum. Upon taking further measurements, one paleontologist thought it looked like it was connected to both the sternum and rib. Could it be the latter? They finally found another specimen whose wing bones did not get fossilized, so they had a good view of the bones on the fossil slab. Two of them were inarguably sternum ribs. It made sense once you saw it, but it required continual data collection and not relying on the first interpretation.

One paleontologist even challenges their intellectual stance by reading the work of creationists. Their anchoring is different, so it raises the question of whether they have seen something differently. Having the discipline to do this depends on your personality, though. You need an open mind and willingness to explore in this manner. Internal debate skills can be cultivated by developing the habit of carving out a fixed time each week to reexamine your analyses and challenge them or to go ask others for their feedback and critiques.

One common theme from the paleontologists and archaeologists is using multiple working hypotheses. As discussed above, multiple different interpretations may be valid (equifinality). Sometimes the hypotheses don't fit—they don't follow the same categories or patterns others have reported. If so, go back to the drawing board and design new hypotheses or collect more data. Archaeologists typically build chronologies on the few sites they study, but expanding the sample to include more sites might show that the chronology doesn't fit (e.g., pottery is from different time periods or is used for different purposes). You will never find a final answer, but it helps narrow the ongoing research frame. Each answer also opens up new questions to explore. Keep challenging yourself to avoid becoming too stale.

Partnering with tribal nations also helps archaeologists develop alternative perspectives because these groups have different questions they want addressed, which ultimately helps the researchers develop insights they would have missed. The tribal nations tend to seek insights connecting them with their ancestors rather than artifacts to be placed in a museum. Archaeologists talk with them at the initial stages of any project to help refine the questions to ask and the data to collect. If they don't, it's much more likely the early efforts at the dig site could preclude a later exploration of the questions the tribes are asking (partly because the process of digging necessarily destroys the original site itself).

These discussions can yield entire research questions the scientists wouldn't have thought of otherwise. One archaeologist shared how talking with Native tribes helped them see the landscape in a whole new way. As one example, the area they were studying was covered with millions of pieces of obsidian lying on the surface from the nearby dormant volcano. It felt like throwaway material, especially because it was so abundant. The tribe wanted to know the history of the landscape and how their ancestors had interacted with it over time. Since obsidian is X-ray fluorescent, the researchers collected samples and found the obsidian came from five different sources. In addition, the intensity of the obsidian use had varied over time, implying the landscape had been used differently by the Natives' ancestors across the years. What looked like uniform detritus was instead a crucial clue to answering the tribe's questions.

Latent bias can also affect our decision-making. Recall the archaeologist from lesson 6 who ignored the old pottery and tools that turned out to be the key to understanding the site. That life lesson has stuck with them, which they impart to their students: it's hard not to fall into a biased way of thinking. A different interviewee instructs their graduate students to maintain a journal they don't share with their advisor. If the lead archaeologist on a dig says a wall is second-century BC, the students should note in their journal if they disagree—and why. This process helps students formulate thoughts without the pressure of an immediate interaction. When the advisor asks if there are other ideas, the students have their journal thoughts to offer. It requires creating a climate where independent thoughts are accepted. If the student disagrees, the advisor has to accept their assertion and ask why. (The interviewee's dissertation advisor wasn't so accommodating, which is probably one of the reasons the interviewee is so diligent about creating that process and space for their own students.)

Large, diverse teams (recall lesson 1) also encourage independent thinking. Working with many different people brings different eyes and methodological viewpoints to challenge the accepted hypothesis. One interviewee's most insightful feedback came from second graders on a tour of a local archaeological site. While describing the work being done at the site, one of the kids asked, "Why?" The archaeologist thought explaining *what* they were doing was also conveying the *why* but evidently not. Children can have a naïve way of looking at the world, but that can be beneficial because they're unburdened by prior beliefs. This simple question from an outsider caused the team to reevaluate if they were asking the right questions themselves as they conducted their research (lesson 2). Listen to a broad range of people even if you think they may have naïve intelligence. Not everyone sees the world the same way, so review things from their perspective.

We have already discussed how we often see our competitors as irrational because they aren't making choices we would if we were them.
That's a biased way of looking at the world. Not everyone *should* be
making the same choices because they have different perspectives,
capabilities, and starting positions. Deliberately give yourself time to
step back and think about the world from someone else's point of view.
Surround yourself with others who can help supportively stress test
your competitive insights by providing different perspectives.

Lesson 9: Understand to Whom You Are Telling Your Story

Even if you can complete the analysis appropriately, if you can't convince other leaders in your organization that you have the correct
insight, your work will have gone for naught. The penultimate lesson
provides advice about how to ensure your message resonates with the
audience you're trying to influence.

The detective had multiple different audiences they needed to
address, from the suspect and witnesses to the attorneys and jury during
trial. Different techniques were used with each audience. For example,
with the suspects, they would keep secret some of the facts, ones never
released to the public. Only the killer or any associates would know
them, which could provide more certainty of the suspect's involvement. (Yes, this classic trick from TV shows and movies actually works!)

The story that will resonate for an individual scientist and the field at
large is also different. A paleontologist was trying to convince the field
of a new interpretation of how a species had evolved. Some paleontologists agreed, but many opposed the new idea. At times, the paleontologist felt like a voice yelling in the wilderness because of the number
who dismissed the idea. Even those intrigued by the hypothesis needed
more data before they'd fully believe it. A turning point came when
another team independently found similar fossils and made a similar
conclusion. The paleontologist paired up with the team, and the collaboration provided support. It ultimately took ten to fifteen years to convince most others, and some never ended up believing the conclusions.

The paleontologist focused on convincing graduate students they worked with since they would grow into the next wave of professors. This helped advance the idea as did convincing the son-in-law of one of the idea's main adversaries. The important end result was that the new idea ultimately became the consensus view. As a strategist, you may not need to initially convince the CEO that the competitor's predicted reactions are the correct ones, but if you can build up enough support with the junior staff that the competitive insights are accurate, they'll consistently use those in their recommendations to their managers. As we'll see in chapter 7, it's important to have senior leadership support for the competitive insight group, but sometimes a groundswell of support from below can turn the direction of the organization.

Another paleontologist discussed the importance of developing peripheral vision, or understanding the perspectives of others who aren't immediately aligned. You have to know enough about the person in the next office even if they research a different topic. They had a postdoctoral fellow who really wanted to get a paper published in *Science*, a highly prestigious journal. The fellow was trying to convince everyone of the importance of their article on its own merits, but the interviewee explained to the postdoc that they had to explain *why* their work was relevant to others. It's not about the importance of a result on its own but how those conclusions would make a difference to others' work. The broader you can make your ideas' relevance to fields beyond your own, the more interest the insights will generate.

One paleontologist and one archaeologist brought up the importance of messaging for securing funding. It's important to highlight the ways the insights are more broadly applicable beyond a narrow niche to generate willingness to contribute resources to support the research.

The NICU nurses shared the importance of understanding the parents' learning needs in order to best communicate with them. It's not about knowing their educational attainment level but understanding *how* they learn—for example, raw data, comparisons, analogies, technical details, or some combination of these. NICU nurses also must know each parent's triggers—the messaging they should avoid. Ultimately, they need to help parents know what is happening and to prepare them for the day the baby is sent home. Information must be communicated in a way that will allow parents to best digest it to ensure their child is well cared for after being discharged.

Competitive insight strategists should also think clearly about how to communicate their findings to the various audiences that matter. Making the process and insights as broadly applicable to different segments of the organization will increase the odds of securing funding from the C-suite. Crafting insights in a way easily digestible by the rest of the organization will improve the chances they are actually used. You need determination to continue sharing the insights in the face of resistance to finally break through to the most intransigent colleagues.

Lesson 10: Remember There Is Always a Driver of the Behavior You Seek to Explain

The final lesson comes from the detective and archaeologists since they're the professionals who investigate and explore adult human behavior. This lesson reinforces all the previous frameworks: the competitor organization is a group of individuals making choices, and their motivations drive their behavior. It may not always be obvious what that motivation is—and you may not perfectly understand it—but it is there in the background.

The detective shared a story of an individual who robbed a bank. Their first thought was there had to be a reason it happened; no one does something like that by accident or without a rationale. The detective asked the suspect, "What happened to you that forced you to do this?" The response was he had to feed his family. The detective replied if that was true, the suspect's family would be brought some food. "Seriously?" asked the suspect. After the detective told him yes, the suspect responded, "OK, I did it and these other crimes." The detective did deliver food to the suspect's family after which the suspect told the entire story: how he had bought snacks but had no more money left for additional food. He also revealed what car was used, where it was, the type of bag, and its location—everything the detective needed to recover the money.

Some behavioral explanations are straightforward. For example, 90 percent of ancient settlements are within a well-determined distance from a water source. There is clearly a reason for this: people had to be close to water to survive. Also, a site on sloping ground often has drainage ditches around the hut, which was used to keep the homes dry. However, sometimes the behavioral explanation is more uncertain. For example, one archaeologist's research explored two sites close to each other. One was eight thousand years old, while the other was four thousand years old. There were commonalities across the sites, such as charred botanical remnants indicating what the societies ate. The archaeologist was interested in whether the societies had organized food production around the household unit or the community as a whole. This was not obvious from the food remnants, but they were able to find evidence for the number of people involved in food production at each site. The evidence showed that everyone worked together in large groups at the earlier site (communal production) but in smaller groups later (household). The behavior within the group influenced the remains found at the two sites.

One interviewee shared an old archaeology joke: if you can't explain why the society behaved in a way that left the remains, then it must have been due to "ritual." That's a true catch-all answer (somewhat like if business leaders can't explain competitors, they're irrational). There is a continuum of obvious to very difficult answers, with differing opinions among archaeologists of what they are even looking at. What is the fragment? What type of structure is being unearthed? What was its function? These can be hard to determine, especially when the preservation isn't good, such as for many functional items.

One area where this behavioral uncertainty arises is with funerals. Archaeologists believe much effort was usually put into burial, which had some sense of ritual, but how could they push the explanation further for why effort was made? For example, how would one explain an expensive item (say, a sword) buried in a tomb? This seems very unwise because now a valuable item can no longer be used by the society. For a metal-poor society in particular, burying metal is definitely not optimizing behavior, but that's taken from the viewpoint of our modern sensibility. Putting an expensive item in a tomb can confer prestige on the family—and the society—relative to others. If there is a public burial to show off what's getting entombed with the deceased, the family's mentality comes into focus. Burying the sword to create prestige is exactly why it looks foolish to us: they are willing and able to relinquish something of such immense value.

Archaeology is a set of nested theoretical layers built up from empirical evidence. The artifacts and distribution of sites on a map all lead back to the behaviors that caused those findings. Any one particular behavior creates many physical traces, and what archaeologists see is a pretty generous subset of that data. Patterns exist in the behavior; the constraint is finding the evidence leading to the underlying cultural phenomenon studied.

Competitive insight yields an understanding of the behavior of other organizations. It may feel sometimes like it's too challenging of an exercise, but this final lesson should reinvigorate your effort. Even though we can only see the pricing, marketing, new product, supply chain, and acquisition choices of the competitors in the real world, there is always a behavior underlying those actions.

Bonus Lessons

There were a few final nuggets from the interviews I wanted to share. These can help create the mindset that allows you to be a better competitive strategist.

- Be humble—you don't know the answer going in.
- Don't make broad sweeping conclusions—stick to what you can say.
- Keep the big picture in mind—your work will be important and provide new insights.

- Don't be afraid to challenge yourself and go outside your comfort zone.
- If you can't be surprised by what you find, then you can't do a good job.
- Finding errors in your work is a source of inspiration.
- Failure is part of the learning process.
- You can't do science until you've done the people work.
- "Obvious" is a flag that others don't know what they're talking about or want to ignore assumptions.

One critique I received from someone who declined to be interviewed was that this is all just basic decision-making. Every decision has an element of uncertainty around it, so there's nothing unique about not being able to talk with a newborn or an ancient civilization or a dead body (human or from an extinct creature). However, after having talked with these two dozen experts, I have come away with a stronger conviction that there is a difference. When you can talk with customers, suppliers, regulators, or partners, there is less urgency about applying these lessons. Additionally, the skepticism surrounding predicting competitors means the analysis needs to be even more certain (like the detective prepping a case for a court trial). The ultimate confirmation came when one of the archaeologists shared that they teach a course at their university on decision-making in fields where you cannot directly interact with the subject. If it's different enough to earn college credit, then we should believe our task as competitive strategists is more complicated than typical decision-making.

Remember, nothing is ever 100 percent provable. There are still mysteries about King Tut's reign or what life was like in Pompeii. And while paleontologists would love to observe living dinosaurs, the *Jurassic Park* movies remain fiction.

I'd like to leave you with one final archaeology story. The first evidence of humans hunting shows cut marks on the thigh bones left behind, so humans were definitely involved. The fleshy, upper hind leg of prey has the most muscle, so were the cut marks evidence that humans were after the muscle? Or were they after the fat? Did they cut the muscle off to feed other animals so they could get at the marrow in the bone? Any of the answers could be consistent with the evidence, so the bone marks don't prove one way or the other what early human hunters were after. It can be so frustrating to archaeologists to never be able to definitely prove their case, but it also drives them to seek more evidence to converge on the best explanation possible. That's ultimately what you're after with regard to your competitors.

6 How Can I Put These Concepts into Practice?

Mark Twain's historical novel *The Prince and the Pauper* is about two young boys living in the sixteenth century. Young Prince Edward grew up in the castles and royal environs of England, while Tom Canty was a poor boy who could only dream of being able to lead the nobles' life of luxury. While Edward has access to every material good that he desires, the lack of freedom to be anonymous grates on him. The twist Twain introduces is that the two boys are doppelgängers, and when they decide to switch places to experience the life each thinks is easier, they soon realize the grass isn't always greener on the other side. Tom understands the weight of royal decisions and the pressures from adults in the court are not easy to deal with. Edward's experiences with Tom's alcoholic father and the abject poverty he sees all around are not easily endured. Both of them can literally experience life while walking in each other's shoes.

Can you, as a business leader, do the same? You can't call up the CEO at your competitor and ask to swap places for a couple of weeks. But there are some techniques you can use to simulate living the life of your competitor. They build upon the work from part II but add an element of interaction to the thinking. I will discuss these in turn, starting with Black Hat exercises and then proceeding to several variations of war gaming. I'll also discuss a few common strategy exercises that aren't really competitive insight tools (though they are helpful in answering different competitive strategy questions).

There are many books and articles on war gaming, and my intention here isn't to reinvent the wheel. I'm going to focus on the basics of what war gaming (and what I'll call, more broadly, competitive insight) exercises are. I'll address how to conduct them in a nonmilitary setting, based on lessons I've learned from doing competitive insight exercises for over fifteen years. I'll also discuss the mindsets and the tips and tricks that help make a particular workshop more successful and insightful. (I will use "exercise" and "workshop" interchangeably. Competitive insight doesn't require a dedicated workshop—it can be as simple as sitting around a conference table discussing the right issues.)

There are three steps to conducting a competitive insight workshop regardless of the specific form:

1. **Design** the exercise.
2. **Build** the content used in the workshop.
3. **Run** the event.

Design: Engage with multiple stakeholders to answer the common "six W" questions: who, what, where, when, why, and how. The stakeholders include the workshop participants, in addition to those who won't attend but nonetheless need to use the information generated. The latter group includes colleagues both upstream (e.g., senior managers) and downstream (e.g., frontline staff) in the organization. Yes, it may seem trite to ask these elementary questions, but there's a reason it's a well-used construct: it works! And in the case of designing a competitive insight exercise, it is very helpful for thinking about the relevant workshop parameters.

- *Who* are the relevant players that need to be role-played? Who will actively influence the decisions our organization has to make, and who will be influenced sufficiently by our decisions so they will change their actions?
- *What* types of choices do we want each of the role-playing teams to make in the exercise? Brainstorming sessions aren't especially helpful if teams can come up with anything they want. Additionally, if the teams focus on different topic areas, you won't necessarily determine

how each team reacts to the choices of others—they might be responsive to each other, or they could talk about completely different strategic levers and decisions. To help focus the teams, develop a short list of topic areas for them to discuss. (You can always include a category for "other" in case the role-playing team decides that a more creative move will win the day.)

- *Where* will the teams' choices be played out? What are the geographic regions, the customer segments, and the industry subsectors the players should be addressing? Again, for players to concentrate on similar areas, you'll need to define these upfront.

- *When* will the choices play out? What is the first time period in the real world for which you will be simulating actions? How many subsequent periods will be covered, and what will be their duration (e.g., quarterly, six months, annual, longer)? The duration and timing depend on the type of decision. For example, large capacity decisions play out over longer time periods than fast-moving consumer goods pricing decisions. You must define the timing so each team will be looking at the same horizon.

- *Why* do role-playing teams care about the simulation outcomes? This overlaps a bit with determining who should be included in the exercise (if the team doesn't care, they probably shouldn't be included). Think about the strategic objective driving each role-playing team.

- *How* will the interactions be evaluated, and how will they produce insights? This final question sets the context for the next step: what set of materials will be used in the actual exercise?

Build: Once you have sketched out the basic framework through the six Ws, you need to build the materials to be used in the workshop. What preread materials will help put the teams in the mindset of the role they'll be playing? Are there worksheets you want them to fill out to document their decisions? What models do you need to build to assess the market outcomes based on the teams' decisions? What presentation materials must be created? When you enter the room for the actual exercise, everything needs to be ready to go so the participants can focus on the decisions they have to make and the insights you want them to develop. When you have everything prepped, you're ready for the next step.

Run: In actual calendar time, this may be the shortest step of the entire process, but in many ways, it is the most important. It's the whole reason you're holding the workshop: test the choices each player makes against the others to generate insights about how competitors will act and react when faced with certain situations. This step includes the interactions of the role-playing teams, which are almost always composed of participants from your organization. Be *very* careful about asking people from other organizations to participate because doing so can expose you to anticompetitive risks. Consult your legal counsel if there's someone external you'd like to invite.

This step also includes the debrief session. In some sense, this is *the* most important part of the whole competitive insight exercise. If you don't allocate time during the workshop to discuss as a team the insights you develop, then there won't be any organizational learning. If you don't debrief the exercise on the same day, individuals may walk away with their own unique thoughts and conclusions. The entire group must leave the exercise with the same insights. You might think it would be better to wait a few days to debrief, giving individuals the opportunity to ruminate on what happened and draw some conclusions. In reality, when people leave the room, they shift back into their "regular day job" mode. They don't set aside time to think about implications from the workshop.

Therefore be sure to conduct the debrief before they leave for the day. You can always follow up a few days or weeks later to build upon those preliminary insights, but have that starting point from the initial debrief. (If you do plan to have follow-up conversations, assign topics to each individual so they're ready to subsequently discuss them). The whole point of the workshop is to generate organizational alignment on the competitors' actions to prepare for addressing the potential threats. Ending the session without agreeing to initial takeaways and next steps is a wasted opportunity—all that work without any documented knowledge to show for it.

Guiding all three steps of the competitive insight exercise process is a fundamental question: what core problem are you trying to solve? Or, put another way, what learning objective do you hope to achieve? All competitive insight exercises allow you to practice strategic decision-making. Research tells us that deliberative practice is the key to expertise: practicing a specific subset of activities (e.g., putting in golf, playing a specific set of measures in a concerto) rather than the entirety (e.g., playing a round of golf, playing the entire concerto start-to-finish). But it's hard to "practice" strategic decisions. How can you practice market entry? You may only have one or two chances to go into a new country in your entire career. And you can't practice entering a market, telling everyone to forget what you just did and reset as if it never happened!

A competitive insight workshop allows you to practice these choices in a risk-free environment. If you choose to enter the "wrong" country in real life, you can't call a "do over" and try again. Customers and competitors won't forget. Entering the "wrong" country in a competitive insight exercise merely means you know not to do it in real life. Your customers and competitors won't know you considered it—and many others in your organization won't even know it was an option. You can run the exercise for multiple different countries, or multiple different go-to-market strategies in a specific country, to home in on the "right" way to enter. Practice may not make perfect, but it's a lot better than not practicing at all!

You *can* run a competitive insight exercise for many decisions and many iterations in the same exercise, but you *should not* do so. It takes time and resources to design, build, and run the various workshops described in this chapter. If you tried to tackle all your strategic decisions using them, you'd find yourself doing nothing but these workshops and blowing through your budget. There is some overlap in effort of taking a European market entry exercise and reformatting it to address entry into Asia, but there is always new content and modifications needed (e.g., potentially different competitors, different market conditions, different decision choices).

So how do you narrow in on the most important issues for which to conduct an exercise? The rule of thumb I start with is this: What decisions keep you up at night? Do you worry about entering a new region because you're unsure whether competitors will block you? Or do you worry that if you invest in a new product, they'll come out with a new one before you—or simply copycat your offering quickly enough to blunt your sales? If someone held a pen over your pink slip, threatening to fire you if you didn't make a selection, for which decision would you say, "Sign away?" These significant and challenging decisions are the ones for which you should run a competitive insight exercise to mitigate some of your uncertainty and let you sleep soundly at night.

Some argue you should start with decisions you're supremely confident about, testing to make sure you aren't blinded to some market force or competitor that will ruin the idea. I'm not in favor of conducting competitive insight exercises for these efforts more broadly because you could be introducing different biases (like confirmation bias) with this approach. The exercise also likely wouldn't make that significant of a change to the preworkshop beliefs, eventually leading others in your organization to think these types of efforts are a waste of time. It may occasionally make sense to stress test relatively certain choices, but the war gaming lite option discussed later would be the avenue to use (and use selectively). In summary, competitive insight exercises should not be used for every decision you make—they would lose their impact as a decision-making tool. Be selective about when and how you apply them.

One final piece of overarching advice is to keep it real! A competitive insight exercise is a simulation, so make it as close as possible to the real world. Off-the-shelf exercises and standardized models are easier and quicker to use, but they tend to produce generic learning among the group. ("Wow, so if we raise price a lot, others will try to undercut us and steal share.") Remember the lessons of deliberative practice: force your team to confront choices and situations they'll face in the real world, not in some hypothetical construct.

Let's examine the particulars of several types of competitive insight exercises. They don't replace the frameworks in the previous chapters; rather, those constructs will be useful as you design, build, and run the workshops. Let's begin with Black Hat exercises.

Black Hat Exercises

In twentieth-century movies based in the American Wild West, it was pretty typical for the good guys to wear white hats and the bad guys to wear black hats. In the days of black-and-white film and television, this was very helpful to understanding which character was on which team, especially during a climactic shoot-out. It got so standardized that writers and directors started putting the good guys in black hats and the bad guys in white ones earlier in the storyline so viewers couldn't guess who was going to win. (Surprise, it was the good guy!) To this day, the mnemonic persists: good guys wear white hats, and bad guys wear black hats.

As a competitive insight exercise, a Black Hat session helps you understand what it's like to wear the competitor's hat (instead of walking a mile in their shoes). The competitor is who you're fighting with for market share and consumer mind space. They're the bad guys hurting your organization. So what's it like to view the world from their perspective? This should sound a lot like the framework in chapter 1, and indeed it does, except the Black Hat session builds upon the ongoing work of understanding the competitor's mindset.

A Black Hat exercise is focused on a particular strategic situation you are facing—for example, your plan to introduce a new product to the market, a competitor's potential entry, or a change in government regulations. In the simplest form, the Black Hat session focuses on role-playing one competitor to analyze how they would approach that circumstance. What I'll describe below are workshops that could also include other organizations, such as additional competitors or your own company. But keep in mind throughout that the Black Hat workshop does *not* need to include these others—you can focus the entire exercise on role-playing one key competitor.

In the Black Hat workshop, the competitor will be role-played to simulate how they will act. Will they be aggressive? What levers will they pull? Will they even be capable of responding to the situation? You can assess how they will react or make a spontaneous move. A Black Hat dives deeper into the particular tactics they'd use than the overall strategy viewpoint developed in chapters 3 and 4. You can also include other competitors and your own organization as players in the exercise, having them address the question, "We think Competitor X is about to enter South America—what would our role-playing team do to make it more difficult for them to be successful if they do enter? And can we deter entry in the first place?"

Design: The design of the Black Hat exercise answers the following questions:

- Who else wears a Black Hat besides our primary competitor? Do we want to role-play them in this session too?

- What types of tactics can the teams choose to execute?

- Where will we focus our discussion geographically, on which customer segments, and in which industry subsectors?

- When will the teams' decisions be introduced to the market (or at least announced)?

- Why is the Black Hat competitor considering this strategic decision (what is their objective?), and how will other players view their potential move?

The "how" question is omitted because a Black Hat exercise doesn't require a formal evaluation of the market outcomes. Most involve only exploring one competitor's mindset and potential strategies. The choices by the one player are not enough to formalize into a market model. (What are the choices of the other market players?) Instead, the Black Hat exercise participants will assess in the debrief how challenging and effective the competitor's strategic choices would be for your organization to contend with. If there are multiple competitors, or you include your organization, you will still assess the effectiveness of each team's choices without a model. If you do need a formal evaluation of the market results, you should run a war game instead. The Black Hat exercise is more strategic than tactical, so you can omit the details of the competitor's payoff. We'll see shortly how the session is run and how the insights regarding impact are generated.

Build: To provide participants with materials that will help them in the workshop, you want to create the following:

- An *industry fact pack* so all the participants are on the same page. You will waste time if teams use different assumptions. For example, if one team assumes average pricing has been declining, while another is playing as if they have been flat, the outcome of the exercise won't reflect real-world choices, so you won't satisfy the learning objective. The fact pack includes all relevant information about the market, such as market shares, average pricing, customer segments, demand growth, key government regulations, and technological changes.

- *Role-playing fact packs* so the teams have a fact base to use when making their decisions. Participants role-playing the competitor teams will often assume they are either overly capable (that's why they're in the Black Hat—you can't seem to beat them) or completely incapable (they're not you, so they can't possibly be as competent). Or there will be disagreements within the role-playing team on their capabilities. For each team, use chapter 1 to assess the following questions: What is their objective, and what has their historical performance been along key metrics? What are the key choices they've made in the past along the dimensions the team will examine in the game? What are the leadership profiles? Provide a fact base that aligns the role-playing team on the resources, assets, and capabilities available for the competitor to use. Create one for each team, including one for the team role-playing your organization (if included). No cutting corners here and assuming that everyone on the team representing your company knows the relevant information about your organization. Putting the information in writing ensures everyone is on the same page.

- A couple of *scenarios* around the question at hand to which the teams have to react: for example, two potential changes foreseen in the industry, a strategic move proposed by your own organization, or upcoming changes to key governmental regulations.

- A common *template* for all the teams to use that contains spaces to note which tactics they will use along each dimension (e.g., price, customer segment, product portfolio, R&D investment, marketing spend). These will help guide the teams to focus on the relevant decisions, not to limit them. Remember to include an "other" category on the template to capture innovative ideas, if desired.

- A scripted *agenda* to ensure everything gets done on time. Key elements include an introduction, timing for each scenario (breakout and plenary discussions), breaks (e.g., for coffee, lunch), and the debrief portion at the end of the session.

The first two items (industry and role-play fact packs) should ideally be shared with each participant a few days before the workshop so that they have time to read and begin to digest. (If there's too much preread time, the documents will sit untouched.) Everyone receives the same industry fact pack (this is public information on the state of the market), but each participant gets only the role-play fact pack for the organization they are simulating in the workshop.

Don't give all the role-play fact packs to every participant! These documents act as "private" information each team has available for itself even though the material in them comes from publicly available sources. (No spying or illegal activity!) In theory, the information is available to anyone, but in reality, we know from having reached this point in the book that most companies don't spend the time researching and creating synthesized assessments of other organizations. Assume the others don't have complete competitive insight assessments for all the players in the exercise. The teams role-playing the competitor organizations shouldn't have that advantage. (Besides, if you give all the role-play fact packs to every participant, the workshop becomes an optimization exercise calibrated against each of the players. This isn't how the real world works—you don't control all the other competitors.)

Provide the prereads on the day of the workshop if you don't think anyone will read them before arriving. Build in extra time into the schedule at the beginning of the workshop for participants to read over the materials in their team rooms.

Run: Establish the session's purpose at the beginning of the day (or days—typically one day will do, but you could run two days if there are enough scenarios and variations to test). Then, have participants break out for forty-five to sixty minutes into individual team rooms to discuss how they would address the issues at hand along the tactics/levers you assign (e.g., product portfolio, price, marketing spend, partnerships). The amount of time depends on the number of decisions you want them to make. Pricing, product portfolio, and distribution channel decisions will take less time than if they also have to determine advertising spend, new product development, and any partnerships.

If a team is role-playing a competitor contemplating a move—say, rumor has it they're planning to enter your geography or introduce a completely new type of product or service—then the team will debate how they would make that move if they ran the company. At the same time, in their own room, the team role-playing your own company would discuss how they think the competitor will enter. They'll debate whether, and how, to blunt that competitor's move. Other teams would role-play the other competitors' actions or those of complementors, platform partners, regulators, significant customers, or distributors.

After all the teams craft their own strategic plans, they'll regroup in the plenary session. Each team will announce their plan, allowing the participants to debrief the implications for the market and their own organization. After all the teams have spoken, they can question each other and probe assumptions and aspects that might have been omitted in the strategy descriptions. For example, let's say your company's team decides they want to lower prices to preserve market share in the face of the competitor's entry. When the competitor team announces their plan, they may not mention pricing, so the company role-playing team should ask what the pricing would be.

What you do *not* want to discuss is the "why" behind each team's choices. Don't pull back the curtain to reveal the underlying objective of each team or the motivation driving the specifics of their plan. You will delve into this at the end of the exercise, but if you do it too early, subsequent workshop scenarios will not allow teams to wrestle with their choices. All the teams will know what each other will do because they'll know the underlying drivers, so they'll be able to counter the others in subsequent rounds.

After the teams have discussed the first set of plans, you can introduce a new scenario. For example, you might ask the teams to consider again a potential entry into the company's core market, but this time under the assumption the economy is entering a recession. The teams would break out into their rooms for forty-five to sixty minutes to explore how they'd attack the market under the new constraints. They'd subsequently gather again in plenary to announce their choices and discuss them.

After all the planned scenarios have been analyzed, the teams remain in plenary to discuss implications and debrief the entire session. I like to begin this phase by asking each team the following three questions:

1. What was your team's objective?

2. What was your most interesting insight about playing your role today, either as it relates to that organization or to the industry overall?

3. What remaining "unknowns" would you like clarified about your role or the industry in order to have better insight?

In other words, what were you trying to do, what did you learn by doing it, and what outstanding questions do you still have? This debrief at the end of the workshop should leave enough time to synthesize takeaway learnings. It should also offer a set of "next steps" for gathering additional information, exploring alternative strategic options, and disseminating the insights to others in the organization. I generally like to leave at least an hour at the end of the workshop for this summative debrief session, but regardless of how much time you leave, be sure you debrief on the day of the workshop—once participants leave, their recall of insights diminishes rapidly.

As an example of a Black Hat exercise, I'll describe one conducted for a consumer electronics company. There were indications a large multinational competitor might enter their geography even though the other company wasn't currently selling the particular product in the region. Some people at the client company thought the competitor wasn't planning to enter (since they hadn't yet), and even if they did, the client would be able to eat their lunch and prevent any large market share impact. As the event unfolded, however, the client understood that despite their self-confidence, the multinational was *very* likely to enter.

The statements the competitor had made about entering were supported by actions taken by the team role-playing them to set up the supply chain and distribution to support entry. The client team's initial strategy proposal to counter the entrant in the workshop was overly confident, making the team sure they would prevent large market share gains. However, in the plenary session announcing the first round of plans, they realized their efforts would have no effect on the entrant. Actually, their actions might even open up entry routes for the competitor that might otherwise have been kept closed. At the end of the workshop, the client's two main insights were "The competitor will almost certainly enter and be a big threat when they do" and "Why can't we start doing what the competitor team planned to do? Let's talk with marketing and sales and operations to see if we can beat them to the punch!"

A second client, in the consumer-packaged goods sector, asked for help understanding any potential gaps in their market entry plans for a new technology they were going to introduce. They'd fallen prey to the common mistaken perspective of "We're introducing something that's really cool, and much better performing, so we'll clearly win in the market." We held a workshop to role-play their two main competitors and a collection of potentially disruptive entrants to the market.

The competitor teams decided to lower pricing, adjust their advertising, tie up large retailers with longer-term contracts, and try to tweak product standard boards. These actions would mitigate many of the client's forecasted gains.

Two of the competitor teams kept asking if they could merge, which we decided against, primarily to keep the exercise engaging for everyone involved. The client concluded they had to better track the competitors' moves to understand which possible reaction they were leaning toward. They also realized the need to undertake additional preemptive actions to blunt those potential competitor moves. When two competitors in the market subsequently did merge in the real world, the client was less surprised. They were also able to use a structured process to assess how that merger would affect the upcoming product launch, building off our previous work.

One final piece of advice is that I would generally not recommend running a Black Hat exercise where multiple teams role-play the same competitor. While this might seem like a great way to get different groups' perspectives on the same company, there's really only downside risk. If the teams come back with different strategic choices, you'll just be confused about which one to believe. (This implies you haven't done enough work using chapter 1's framework to get information about the competitor.) If they all come back with the same suggestions, then it will feel like the other teams' time was wasted (it could have been used to gain insight into another organization). The only time this could be productive is when you're running a Red Team stress test exercise, which is discussed near the end of this chapter.

Black Hat exercises are a great way of getting into the mindset of other players in the market. You can view the industry from another's perspective without requiring a lot of preparation. The workshops also offer a more realistic discussion of how the sector may evolve compared to sitting around a table discussing how you *want* the industry to evolve. Black Hat exercises can also be used as prework to a war game since they help teams understand the best strategies for their role-play assignment. Let's turn to that type of exercise next.

War Game Exercises

If a Black Hat exercise doesn't provide sufficient insight into the competitor, the next step is to run a war game, which migrated to the business world from military applications. For centuries, armies have simulated how a battle might play out before actually engaging with the other side. A military war game involves a country (and its allies) splitting up to role-play themselves and the enemy forces. Both sides are given instructions on the assets and resources they have at their disposal (like step 2 of our chapter 1 framework) as well as the context of where and when the battle will occur. They then engage in a simulated battle—usually without live ammunition—to test different tactics. Should we attack from the front or the side? Should we advance in waves or all at once? How will the enemy use their tanks and helicopters? Do the answers depend on how we attack? After the exercise in the field, military leaders debrief to understand what worked, what didn't, and what could be done differently to achieve a better outcome.

A business war game is fundamentally the same. You and your competitors are the combatants, with other stakeholders playing supporting roles. The market is the battlefield where you are competing. The assets and resources at your disposal are product portfolios, production facilities, and partnerships (among others). Tactics include pricing, marketing, innovation and R&D, and operational efficiency efforts.

Some pundits argue that this concept of war gaming is antiquated because business is not about cutthroat competition where you must defeat the other side. But that's a very narrow view of what a war game is. At its core, it is a simulated exercise that allows an organization the opportunity for focused practice of its strategic (and sometimes tactical) decisions in a risk-free environment before having to commit to those choices in the real world.

Notice that nowhere in the definition is the word "competitor" used. Therefore let's break the description down because understanding it thoroughly is critical.

- *Simulated*: You are not making choices in the real world; you are recreating an environment as closely as possible to what the real world is.

- *Organization*: This can be the military (where it originated), a for-profit company, a nonprofit, a social group, a government agency, a large established multinational, a local start-up, or an industry association. Business war games can be used by any type of organization.

- *Focused*: Select a small set of choices, not every possible one the company could make, for example, pricing, marketing spend, and customer segment or warehousing, distribution partnerships, and geography.

- *Practice*: World-class experts engage in thousands of hours of dedicated practice to hone their craft.[1] Unfortunately, you can't "practice" business decisions through your normal day-to-day work because you're making those choices in the real world. You don't have the ability to set the constraints on when, where, and how you'll make those decisions in a repeated manner. And thousands of hours implies multiple years of practicing the same decisions—in most organizations you'll have either been promoted (so you're making new decisions) or you'll have left.

- *Risk free*: If you make a catastrophic decision that could bankrupt the entire company in a war game, no one outside the room has to know. Investors won't know. Competitors won't know. Others in the organization won't necessarily know. Bad decisions have no consequences in this setting—other than the educational benefits they impart, which are extremely valuable.

A war game allows you to practice a series of business decisions that focus on the key uncertainties creating risk for the organization. Just like Serena Williams practices just serves, volleys, and then backhands (focusing her time on one skill then the next and within the context of a potential match situation), you should ideally focus on marketing, operations, and then industry strategy. If Serena makes a mistake while practicing drop shots or slice backhands, the Wimbledon organizers are not going to revoke her invitation. Similarly, you won't be fired for bad outcomes in a war game, but the more you practice the uncertain situations you face in the marketplace, the better you'll be able to make decisions in the real world when necessary.

War gaming helps test your new-found skills generated in a Black Hat exercise too. Think of Black Hat workshops as step 0 of a war game: who are your competitors, and why do they behave the way they do? Remember, Black Hat exercises are applicable to complementors, platform partners, regulators, distributors, customers, or suppliers. The same is true for war games: any type of player in the industry can be included as long as they are a player whose actions affect your organization and who are directly affected by you in return.

Now that we've discussed the concept, let's explore how to actually put this into practice. There are two primary forms a war game can take; we'll start with the more traditional one.

A Full-Blown, Military-Style Logistics Affair

Like a military war game, the organization divides itself into groups representing itself and other stakeholders (e.g., competitors, suppliers, distributors, platform partners, regulators). The teams are tasked with a set of choices to make and objectives to achieve. They all make choices along the dimensions they've been asked to consider, and then the selections are combined and evaluated against each other to determine the market outcome. In the spirit of their military origins, most business war games are typically set up with lots of logistic support and formalized, structured choices and evaluation methods, including

- individual team rooms for each organization represented in the workshop
- templates the teams fill out with their choices for each round
- computer models to help the teams make their decisions, and
- separate computer models to evaluate the outcome.

These games can focus on tactical choices (e.g., specific pricing levels, product attributes, allocation of marketing spend, individual distribution channel outlets), though more commonly, they focus on strategic choices (e.g., pricing policies as opposed to specific levels, business model structures, broad geographic market choices, capacity changes). Regardless of the exercise's objective, the workshop still needs to follow the three steps outlined above: design, build, and run.

Design Designing the game starts with a similar exploration of the game's end as we saw with the Black Hat workshops. What is the learning objective? What information do you want the organization to take away from the exercise? These answers are often gleaned by asking the "simple" question posed earlier of the senior leader in charge of the division running the game: "What is the decision (or set of decisions) keeping you up at night?"

Big decisions with large downsides can have a devastating impact on a leader's career. With their many uncertainties and complex interactions between industry players, they are ideal for war games since Black Hat exercises don't allow you to explore those interdependencies. They're exactly the kinds of choices most leaders feel unable to easily address—partly because they're decisions rarely made, with little opportunity to practice making them.

Once you've determined the learning objective, you can move backward to determine the set of decisions to be made and which ones will result in the learning outcome. The following are some examples of questions to ask:

- Do we need to consider the impact of pricing across competitors?
- Which distribution channels are being used?
- How will marketing spend support those choices?
- Can innovative products shift the outcome?

The answers to these questions become the set of choices the teams will wrestle with in the war game workshop.

Next, similar to Black Hat exercises, you have to think about the market conditions that will constrain those choices:

- Where will these interactions play out geographically?

- What is the relevant time period over which the choices will matter?
- Are there particular customer segments where these interactions will be both critical and difficult to predict?
- Similarly, are there sets of products and services where the competitive dynamics will be most relevant?

These market conditions can be thought of as the game board on which the exercise will be played, while the choices are the actions the players take during the workshop. You must also decide how much time players have to make a move and how long to play the game.

What this is, really, is applied game theory. I know game theory has a bad reputation in the business community. It has promised strategic insight for decades, and yet leaders feel it has underdelivered. Bain & Company's biannual survey, "Management Tools & Trends," once listed game theory as a top tool, but in the last decade, it has not even cracked the top twenty-five analyzed by the firm.[2] I contend there are two reasons for this:

1. Senior leaders think of game theory as simply the "prisoner's dilemma." Virtually everyone who's been exposed to game theory has studied the prisoner's dilemma (I say "virtually" to hedge my bets—I'd actually bet everyone reading this book who's studied game theory knows of this game). The problem is the prisoner's dilemma is a very particular type of game. It does *not* represent all the real-world situations! It's a game in which players make choices at the same time, have symmetric options and objectives, and would be better off cooperating but can't stop themselves from "cheating" on each other. The prisoner's dilemma works for some situations—like price wars—but not for games where players move sequentially (one after the other). It also doesn't immediately apply to games where players have different objectives, different strategic options, or where there isn't an optimal cooperative outcome. Trying to shoehorn every strategic situation into the prisoner's dilemma structure is doomed to fail. Because most leaders equate game theory with the prisoner's dilemma, they are highly disillusioned about game theory in general.

2. If leaders do move beyond the prisoner's dilemma, they often ask academic game theoreticians to help analyze their situation. While I know the academic game theory community does outstanding work, and has helped advance our understanding of strategic interactions, they're not always the best at applying game theory in the real world. Academics typically begin by assuming the structure of the game and then show what the solution is. In the real world, you can't assume the game you're playing. Your task is to figure out the *actual* game you're playing.

How does war gaming, as applied game theory, overcome these problems? First of all, no one would war game the prisoner's dilemma. It's not interesting to simulate with multiple people over the course of a day, especially because we know what the outcome will be. More importantly, designing the war game *is* the task of defining the game you play. It forces your organization to describe systematically the structure of the game, making it more effective than a prepackaged, off-the-shelf game that makes certain assumptions not relevant to your situation.

Game theory is very helpful when thinking about strategic interactions—that's why it was created in the first place! Pure theorists assume the five factors detailed below and then solve the game, while an applied/real-world game theorist must define these dimensions. As the war game is played during the workshop, the "solution" will be clarified. The five key questions are the same ones we saw in chapter 3 when analyzing how a competitor will respond:

- *Who are the players?* Who are the organizations and groups interacting with each other? In the beauty care industry, for example, it could include L'Oréal and MAC but possibly also Avon and Sephora and maybe even regulators (if the issue is new product introduction). There is no need to have multiple competitors if you think they will all behave the same way (i.e., make the same choices). There isn't any additional learning gained from having extra teams compared to the cost of having a team role-play them. Choose competitors that are going to behave asymmetrically to others. Each role-playing team should have three to six members. If there are fewer than three, there usually isn't any debate, but if there are more than six, then one person tends to dominate the discussion, also curtailing debate. Align the number of teams with the number of participants you can (and want to) invite to the workshop.

- *What do they want?* What are each of the players trying to achieve? We can apply our chapter 1 framework here to think about what the various players are trying to do. They might have goals such as maximizing profits (a sensible place to start) but might be focused on market share instead. They might differ with regard to the time period over which they are seeking those objectives. Or they could be pursuing other, nonfinancial metrics.

- *What can they do?* What choices does each player have? Companies can choose various levers to pull: pricing, marketing spend, R&D (e.g., product/process innovation), capacity, partnerships, and so forth. Identify the actual choices players will be making in the real world and include those in the game, not some idealized choices. Be sure to give the teams multiple options; otherwise, they'll simply choose the only option given, which can bias your insights. For example, if they only have the choice of raising prices, they'll opt to raise prices—often for the simple reason that they'd be bored playing the game otherwise.

- *What do they know?* The game's options are also subject to industry-specific and governmental rules and what each player knows about those rules and the overall game, which is the next dimension. The rules governing the play of the game can be expanded to include all information about the game and about each player—including what each player knows about the game and the others. Governmental regulations are obviously rules that must be followed. For example, in most countries companies can't talk with competitors to jointly set prices. The rules of your game include defining who moves when (e.g., at the same time or one after the other) and what each player knows about the others' choices (e.g., do you see their actual price, an approximate price, or just the change in your market share?).

- *What do they get?* What are the outcomes for the players at the end of each round? The payoffs are fundamentally tied to the player's objectives. If a team is trying to maximize market share, their payoff should be measured in market share—not profits. The rules of the game also affect the payoffs. For example, market share allocation differs across industries based on how customers compare prices. Sometimes comparisons are based on absolute price differences, and sometimes customers make relative price comparisons. In some sectors, the impact of a price difference is capped at some level and lowering prices further doesn't lead to additional market share gains. And in some markets, quality differences could negate any price gap, while in others quality differences only moderate the effect of a price disparity. Whatever the rules of the industry may be for how market share is allocated, and to a lesser extent how profits are computed, the calculation rules need to be fleshed out so each player will see the relevant payoff measures they are pursuing.

As an example, a health-care company was considering acquiring a provider in a particular state. The game question was not "how will competitors respond?" (which was too vague and abstract) but "how will this affect our negotiations with payors and other providers, and how will this affect competition in other states?" We designed an exercise in which the client and a competitor team simultaneously negotiated with payors and other providers (e.g., doctor groups). We then provided the teams with a role-play deck that included their objective (in this case, a mix of profitability and market share). The two providers had to choose which doctor networks to build and which services to focus on as well as which states to compete in.

To help with the learning objective, we picked one state where the client was strong, one where the competitor was strong, and one where they were balanced. The payors and doctor groups then had to choose which provider to partner with and agree to the deal terms. All the groups had some information about the choices the others were making, but they didn't have complete information because it takes time in the real world to see exactly what others have actually decided to do. After all the negotiations were completed, each player was given their market share and profitability outcomes. The game helped the client address their learning objectives: Who got the best deal, and, more importantly, what does the best deal look like? What did the counterparties respond to? How were we able to learn what the competitor was offering? And what was the right order in which to approach payors and providers?

This process is practical applied game theory; it's not an off-the-shelf game. It's based on the actual world and situation the organization is facing and is designed to replicate that world as closely as possible, allowing the optimal practice experience. It's also for those situations where strategic interactions matter because no focus group could assess how the competitor will likely behave, and if you simply ask individuals in your organization to forecast the competition without role-playing them, they'll usually default to "they're not a threat" or "they're too irrational to predict."

Build The time it takes to build the war game depends on several factors. Just as there is no one-size-fits-all game design, there is no standard length required to build a game. But there are some key elements that must be built, like the ones needed for a Black Hat exercise.

- *Role-playing fact packs*: These are the same as the ones built for a Black Hat exercise. Only share these with the participants role-playing that particular player.
- *Industry fact pack*: This is also the same as the ones for a Black Hat. As long as the information is necessary for making choices in the game, it should be included. If it's not helpful or relevant, leave it out. (This also applies to the role-playing fact packs.) Everyone needs to be playing off the same fact base. The only reason to allow teams to use different assumptions would be if you believe the various players hold different beliefs in the real world. If that's the case, include suggested assumptions in their role-play decks.
- *Decision templates*: These are the same as for a Black Hat exercise. They also serve as the teams' submissions at the end of each round.

- *Decision-making calculator*: This is a pro forma spreadsheet to help the teams perform basic P&L calculations. The players enter information from the decision template into the spreadsheet. The calculator estimates profits, market shares, and other objective-based metrics to help the team make decisions. You should build this calculator so that the participants spend time on debating choices, not on crunching numbers on a scratch pad.

- *Agenda*: To determine the length of time needed for the entire workshop, first decide how many games to play and how long each round within the games needs to be. Most war games require scheduling one or two full days. Less than one day isn't enough to run more than one game and have sufficient time for debriefing, and more than two days can run the risk of the event becoming tedious for the participants. War games take longer to run than Black Hat exercises because the latter do not have multiple rounds per scenario. As we'll see below, each war game scenario involves three breakout rounds, which can take half a day or more to complete in total. Each Black Hat scenario should take about one and a half to two hours: forty-five- to sixty-minute breakouts and forty-five- to sixty-minute plenary discussions.

- *Facilitator's guide*: As consultants running games for clients, we would often have members of the firm sit with each of the role-playing teams, while others would float around helping with logistics and keeping things on track. If you plan to have individuals in these roles, you should enumerate the basic ground rules (e.g., don't solve the problem for the role-playing team, but ask probing questions to push their thinking).

If your organization wants to test a specific set of choices at a more tactical level, you'll need to build a computer model. It will take the teams' choices and assess outcomes on the metrics of note for the teams, such as market share and profitability. Games with computer models typically require six to eight weeks to build, depending on the programming complexity involved. Avoid the temptation to make the model as detailed as possible. It should follow this simple design formula:

1. Define the choices the players will make.
2. Determine the outcome metrics of interest for assessing player performance.
3. Build the model to link (1) and (2), nothing more.

Overcomplicating the model creates the impression of precision, which is almost certainly false. It's virtually guaranteed you will make unintended "errors" in your calculations and assumptions, and a false sense of certainty in the outcomes will arise. It's perfectly acceptable to have models and to make predictions, but they should always be couched in the level of uncertainty surrounding the situation. As mentioned above, war games are inherently about assessing uncertain situations, not those with precise, predictable outcomes.

The alternative to using a computer model to determine the results would be having a panel of experts assess the teams' submissions and assign outcomes based on their knowledge of the market. The panel should include three to five members to ensure a robust discussion and debate of the outcomes, thereby avoiding potential bias. A panel is especially useful for more qualitative games not easily modeled with a computer. I've conducted games where the panel assigned plusses or minuses to the team's choices to represent the relative impact, and those with the most plusses and fewest minuses were declared the winner.

Finally, you will need to decide the number of games and rounds within each game. What this means is best described with an example and a visual (see figure 6.1). Say you are trying to assess the market entry and growth strategy for a new country where your organization currently doesn't have a presence. You might want to assess how to enter in case the country's economy grows at the current rate or 3 percent faster, or you might want to assess how to play against only local competitors or local and other multinational entrants. Each scenario would be its own individual game, covering the same time period and with the same core set of choices (modified slightly for each game's context).

Within each game, you would have multiple rounds (three is optimal in my experience; in the first-round teams make choices, in the second

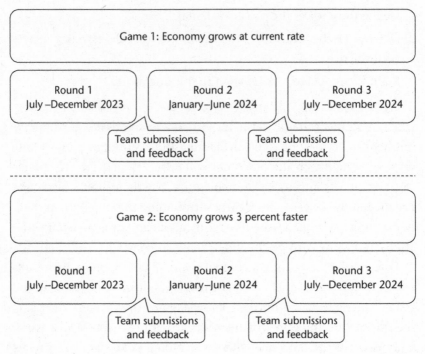

Figure 6.1
Example design of a war game's flow

round they react to the other teams, and in the third round they get to respond to the other players' reactions) that cover the relevant time periods. In this case, you might have round 1 cover the next six months, round 2 focus on months seven through twelve, and round 3 cover months twelve through eighteen. The length of each round depends on the number and complexity of choices the teams must make: more, and more complex, choices need more time. Usually, I've found that one to two hours is a good starting place, but you can stress test this when developing the game by having a team play the game for one round and see if they could get through all the decisions in the time allocated. (I set the timing for each round to be about five to ten minutes fewer than needed to comfortably make the choices: I want players to feel a bit of pressure—so their attention doesn't wander to emails—but not so hectic they just make guesses to complete the template.)

At the end of each round, teams would make their decisions, submit their template of choices, and receive feedback from the model or expert panel. The feedback would set the starting conditions for each subsequent round. After playing the first game, you would reset—putting aside the outcomes of the first game and starting over with a second game (with a faster growth rate in our example). You can keep repeating this process for new scenarios that would be context for additional games.

Each subsequent game can alter the initial conditions (like faster growth) or can add one more level of complication. Continuing the example from above, a third game might keep a 3 percent growth rate and add a change in regulatory requirements for foreign entrants, while a fourth game might add a shift in consumer preferences away from your company's offering. By adding complications step by step, participants will be able to connect what changed in that version of the game with the new outcome, which will enhance their learning. It is easier to correlate the context changes with outcome changes if only one condition adjusts each time, therefore leading to a better understanding of how differences in the environment affect the organization's outcomes.

Building a game involves putting the nuts and bolts in place so the day (or days) of the actual war game workshop will generate as much insight as possible. We turn to that step next.

Run At its most basic level, running the game is executing the agenda laid out in the build stage. Keep the players on track and make sure they use the materials they were given to make their decisions. You want them to act as faithfully as possible to how the competitors (and other players in the game) would behave in the real world. You are trying to simulate the market, so if they behave opposite to the role-play card your organization won't be able to practice the optimal decisions. However, there are two key points about the day-of workshop that deserve some attention.

First, be careful about trying to script the insights and answers ahead of time. Don't guide the teams to predetermined outcomes. One reason war games are uncomfortable for many leaders is because the exact outcome is often uncertain upfront. Remember how we said that designing the exercise was the same as describing the game (which academics assume)? Well, running the war game is analogous to "solving" the game. If you truly knew what the game's outcome would be, you wouldn't need the time and expense of building and running the game. But rest assured that games will rarely result in a wildly unrealistic outcome. The overwhelming majority of games I've run with clients ended with them saying "that is exactly how the competitors will react, and the outcomes make a lot of sense. Now we know what we need to do to maximize the chances of success."[3]

An example of this came with a war game we built and ran for a defense contractor. In it, we were helping the contractor determine how the US Department of Defense (DoD) was going to manage its weapon system acquisitions in the coming years. As we played the game, the DoD team made a decision that was *not* what we expected. The firm's partner on the project thought the game was wrong and that we had made a fundamental mistake in the design and build stages that would invalidate any insights and erode client goodwill. But we stepped back and thought about why the DoD team made their unexpected decision. We realized it was actually a *very* realistic option for them and a *very* smart move if done in the real world. The learning and insight for the client was *huge* because they realized there was a chance the acquisition game could fundamentally shift to one where the client had to build more partnerships to secure future bids. If we had prevented the DoD team from making their choices by attempting to script the outcomes, we would have missed this important insight.

The second key point is that, similar to the Black Hat exercises, the debrief session at the end of the workshop is as important, if not more so, than the actual game play itself. The debrief time is when all the lessons from the day are synthesized, with next steps agreed upon and assigned. As described above, you must conduct the debrief during the workshop. I usually suggest leaving at least one hour, and more often ninety minutes, for the debrief session. Give everyone ample time to contribute and debate without bogging down the discussion into irrelevant minutiae.

I like to start the debrief session by asking each team to answer the same three questions I use in the Black Hat exercises. I go around the room and capture this input before opening the floor to debate and discussion. This way, we get those first initial thoughts before getting sidetracked by follow-up questions. It provides space for participants reticent to speak up, and it can also reduce groupthink because the input occurs before any group consensus emerges.

Again, these three questions are the following:

- What was your team's objective? This was provided to each team in their role-play fact pack, so the other teams won't know this information for certain. They may have guessed what it was during the game play, but it's good to get it clearly laid out.

- What was your most interesting insight about playing your role today, either as it relates to that organization or to the industry overall? The competitor teams were looking at the market through someone else's eyes, while the team role-playing your organization was unconstrained by "normal" processes.

- What remaining "unknowns" would you like clarified about your role or the industry to have better insight? War games involve uncertainty, and not all of it can be resolved in the workshop. Create a list of knowledge gaps to fill after the event.

These three questions are a great way to start generating insights. And even if the full debrief session doesn't answer all the outstanding issues, having these three questions documented will make it easier to reevaluate the learnings at a future date, if necessary.

One innovation the virtual world has provided is an ability to use virtual whiteboard software to capture participants' thoughts during the debrief. For one recent game, we set up a template with columns for the three questions. We added a fourth column for the participants to enter their thoughts on the implications for the client's strategy. The templates had separate rows for each role-playing team, with color-coded box outlines to differentiate between them. As we moved through the debrief, players on each team posted thoughts using virtual stickies in the appropriate boxes. It was a great way of capturing simultaneous feedback from everyone without fear of groupthink bias. It also provided an instantaneous written record the client could return to in the weeks ahead to recall what they learned (which they subsequently did). The game itself was also virtual, but there isn't any reason virtual whiteboards can't be used for gathering in-person feedback before opening things up to a group discussion. The biggest advantage over a physical whiteboard is the information typed in is stored digitally—no one has to take a photo to capture the ideas. Transcribing from the virtual whiteboard is as easy as cutting and pasting.

I've run games completely in person or fully virtual because hybrid structures do not work. Typically, before the pandemic, all the games I ran were in person. It's a great way to build camaraderie and create organizational alignment by colocating everyone. Every once in a while, we'd have someone who couldn't attend who would ask to phone in (this was pre-Zoom days). They almost always were relegated to being nonentities in the discussion (even in team breakout rooms). I would strongly advise to have everyone in person or everyone virtually logged into the event.

One final piece of advice about the workshop itself is don't be beholden to models, data, and numbers. The outcomes of the war games I remember best had everything to do with bigger strategic moves, not whether the final price in the market was €4.99 or €5.99. My memories involve answering strategic questions: Did teams try to acquire other companies? Did smaller competitors add capacity and price lower than larger players? Did the government decide to buy all their weapons from the same supplier or multiple ones? Did R&D investment make a difference, or was success based on price competition? Models are helpful and can provide useful grounding to the exercise, but don't get lost in them. They can create false precision and overconfidence in a "right" answer the game happens to yield. It's better to focus on the more qualitative insights regarding the important drivers of success in the market. These qualitative insights can often be derived through the second form of war game workshops, which we'll turn to next.

War Gaming Lite

The second format is what I call war gaming lite. In many ways, it's very similar to a traditional war game, especially in its design phase, but there are some key differences in the build and run steps. The best way to describe it is to compare it to the difference between *playing* a game (traditional war game) and *teaching someone* to play a game.

As a reminder, in a traditional war game, players have their own team rooms and proprietary fact packs for the role they're playing. They don't know the other teams' objectives until the debrief session, and they don't have complete information on what the other players have in their arsenal. This setup is analogous to poker (e.g., cards are hidden from each other, and you don't know if the other players are bluffing or have a great hand).

The setup is also similar to board games, such as Clue, which I was recently teaching my kids to play. In that game, three cards—one for the murderer, one for the weapon, and one for the location—are placed in an envelope. The rest of the people/weapon/location cards are shuffled and dealt to the players, which they keep hidden. Over the course of the game, each player guesses who they think committed the murder, with which weapon, and in which location. Other players must show them a card in their hand if it matches the guess, which helps the player guessing to figure out which cards *aren't* in the envelope. You can guess cards that you don't have, or you can guess some cards that you *do* have in your hand. If your guess includes a person and location matching cards you hold, then if no one can show the weapon card, it must be in the envelope. Once a player has seen enough of the other players' cards, she makes a final guess of what's in the envelope and will win the game if she's correct. Playing Clue is a very good parallel to the traditional war game construct.

When I was teaching my kids to play the game, they were clueless on how to proceed (pun intended!). So I did what you normally do when teaching someone to play a game for the first time: we played a couple of times with all the cards exposed. I showed them how to mark the cards they were holding on their tracker sheet and how to choose which cards to show the others. I helped them understand how to move around the board to learn new information, and I explained how to guess cards they held to bluff others and learn even more. I also demonstrated who had to show what as the game progressed—we even took the opportunity to reverse some of the moves to try them again. Once my kids got the grasp of the basics, we played while they kept their cards and tracker sheets hidden.

Teaching my kids how to play Clue is analogous to war gaming lite. Players take time to go to a team room and discuss their team's situation (like looking at the cards in your hand) and then rejoin the other teams in the plenary room. The plenary discussion is conducted by going around the table and asking each player what they planned to do, allowing for a short Q&A on each team's announcement. After every team has had a chance to speak, the discussion goes around the room again. This time, the teams discuss how they would react to what they've heard. They can also ask to go back and change what they wanted to do. The teams can also ask the others why they chose certain moves over others (just like I did when teaching Clue), though the other teams shouldn't completely reveal their objectives until the final debrief is held.

Design: This is done in essentially the same way as a traditional war game. Ask who the players are, what they want, what they can do, what they know, and what metrics matter for assessing their performance. The primary difference is that each team can have one to three players, which allows for either a smaller group or more roles represented in the exercise. There can be fewer players because the rest of the plenary group can provide pushback on any team's choices, resulting in the necessary debate over the best option.

Build: You will need to create role-playing fact packs, the industry fact pack, the decision templates (to help focus the teams' internal discussions), the agenda, and the facilitator's guide. You'll also need to determine how many games to play but not the rounds within each game. The sequential nature of the rounds is incorporated into the round-robin plenary discussion.

If you think competitors and the others role-played in the exercise have "irrational" tendencies, try to create games (situations) that naturally lead them to invoke those choices. You'll be able to stress test those irrational tendencies in each game discussion by going back, changing your action, and seeing if they respond in the same irrational way. You can probe why they make those choices in the plenary session (and to some degree, in each breakout team discussion).

In most cases, you won't need to build a pro forma calculator or a model to calculate outcomes. You can create a simple model for guidance in the plenary and debrief discussions on the likely outcomes, but typically this isn't necessary and leads to debate about the appropriateness of the model rather than the insights from the discussion. Building models generally accounts for the biggest time commitment in a traditional war game process. This is where most of the time savings come from in building a lite war game.

War gaming lite focuses on the qualitative and strategic competitive dynamics and evolution of the industry. A model won't help because the learnings are about where threats are coming from, the typical levers that will get pulled, and whether the situation will naturally deteriorate or stabilize. These insights and outcomes are the natural result of the plenary discussions during the workshop.

Run: The workshop itself is logistically less challenging. You will need fewer support materials, but you'll still need to keep players on track and adhering to the agenda. As explained above, you'll give the players time to discuss their team's strategy in private. The rest of the session occurs primarily in the plenary room, with each team "wearing the hat" of the role they're playing. (Notice the analogy to the Black Hat exercises.) Set aside at least one hour for the final debrief session, where everyone takes off their role-playing hat and approaches the discussion from the perspective of your organization: what have we learned, and what are the next steps?

This may still be a bit confusing to understand, so I'll offer another perspective. I like to position war gaming lite as similar to gathering a group of colleagues to discuss what's going to happen in the future of the industry. Often, these conversations are biased toward what you *want* to have happen in the future. This includes the moves you'd like the competitors to take, the assumption that your moves will be *highly* effective, and a rosy picture of how well things will turn out. A lite war game has the same "future of the market" discussion, but each person at the table approaches the conversation from the perspective of the organization they represent. If representing a competitor, what do they want? If a regulator, which moves will they want to take and which can they take? Or as a distributor, what alternatives do they have?

These debates are less biased because each person is trying to do the best for themselves, wearing the hat of the organization they are role-playing. They are not trying to help the others win; they're trying to help themselves win—until the debrief portion, when everyone puts on the hat of your organization and discusses the exercise's implications. Instead of debating future industry dynamics and framing everything in the best possible way for you, the lite war game reveals likely choices when everyone is trying to do the best for themselves. And that's what happens in the real world.

These are not "mini" war games; they are not smaller versions or about smaller issues. Often, the issues are much bigger picture kinds of things (e.g., changing industry trends, shifts in technology, impacts of geopolitical events). Lite war games are almost always strategic in nature rather than tactical, similar to the strategic nature of Black Hat exercises. (It's difficult to address highly tactical questions in a war gaming lite format.) While the Black Hat workshops help you understand one particular competitor's potential strategic moves, the lite war game helps you understand the potential dynamics between your organization and multiple competitors (and others in the ecosystem). They help you debate whether to change the pricing structure, not the specific pricing level.

Lite war games are great for capability building. They help you think like your competitors, embedding the chapter 1 mindset. Setting up periodic lite war games helps you be more objective and less biased when debating industry evolution. You could hold these discussions every quarter, when your team talks about industry changes and what they're observing that's new. The discipline of repeating these exercises also helps ensure you're constantly updating information and insights on competitors. Each person in your group can be assigned to track their role-play assignment between sessions and come prepared to wear that hat during the debate. You don't have to set aside a whole day for this. Take one hour to talk about the key future uncertainty you're facing that quarter, with everyone wearing their role-play hat. If you're facing a competitor that has made a confusing real-world move, you'll know who to ask—with their role-play hat on—why it was done. You can reassign who tracks which competitor every year or so to keep things fresh and to incorporate new perspectives.

Lite war games also help uncover potential actions your organization might be able to take, similar to what we saw in the Black Hat exercise. Viewing the world from someone else's perspective can free the mind from the constraints of "how we normally do things."

Over time, I've found more and more value in the war gaming lite model. Set up a fact base on the market, assign teams, provide them with a small set of four to five strategic levers, and then jointly discuss how the industry will evolve, with each participant taking the perspective of a different role. Follow-on work will help you narrow in on any detailed models to build and which issues and dimensions are the most important ones requiring more specificity. Losing the forest for a really accurate description of the trees will often result in your standing and admiring a specific Japanese flowering ash yet missing the fact that emerald ash borers are bearing down and will soon destroy the whole forest. War gaming lite helps you rise up above the treetops to see those threats—and potential opportunities.

Four Questions to Ask

Before you decide to design, build, and run a war game (traditional or lite), there are four questions you should ask first.[4]

1. Is a war game the best tool?

    War games are most useful when there are relatively big uncertainties in the market that are not easily quantified, with a wide range of potential outcomes, *and* when the market participants' choices are interdependent (i.e., they are reacting to each other). If competitors appear to be irrational, this is also a good time to war game them out because as we've seen repeatedly, companies aren't irrational—you just haven't figured them out yet.

2. What is the objective of the exercise: strategic or tactical?

    If the objective is strategic, consider using the war gaming lite format. If it's tactical, a traditional war game would be more appropriate. But be clear upfront about the learning objectives, regardless of the workshop format, and how detailed you need to be to reach the desired insights.

3. Who will design, build, and participate in the workshop?

    Make sure you have the right people in the room and assigned to the right roles. Often, those who design the exercise don't play the game since they've peeked behind the curtain of the game's construct. Make sure you have enough dedicated resources to build the game, especially if you are conducting a traditional game and building a model. Be sure you have the right people in the room for the workshop itself, and consider whether you need to draw folks from different divisions, different functions, and different levels of seniority. Deliberately assign participants to each role to maximize the learnings by mixing seniority, experience, and perspectives.

4. How often should we play?

    Traditional war games don't need to be played that often. Typically, they're only used when a major change is occurring in the industry or when your organization is considering a major strategic change. Lite war games can be conducted more frequently, as described above, and can even be ad hoc exercises when needed. They can also be used to highlight the time for a more complex, traditional war game session to dig into the details.

War games, and game theory in general, often have a bad reputation with business leaders. But if you approach them as "describing" a game instead of applying a preset "solution" to the game, you will find them much more insightful.

Other Competitive Insight Workshop Formats

I'd like to highlight two additional competitive insight tools that are similar to war games. Mock negotiations are a very specific format of a war game, while premortems are sometimes referred to as "reverse" war games.

Mock Negotiations

A mock negotiation lets you simulate and practice upcoming negotiations by having someone role-play the counterparty. Having someone filling their shoes will help give better feedback on questions such as the following:

- Are we getting our point across?
- Did we seem too aggressive? Not aggressive enough?
- Is the conversation advancing the discussion, bringing us closer to a conclusion?

The design, build, and run steps are duplicates of the ones seen above.

Design: The players are you and the counterparty. You still need to determine the objectives for the other side and to specify the objectives you want, so they're clarified in everyone's mind. The choices your side and the counterparty can make in the workshop are the terms and conditions and any other dimensions you're negotiating in the real-world contract (e.g., pricing, contract length, product and services included).

Build: As before, you'll need role-playing and industry fact packs. These should concentrate on the issues at the heart of the contract. The decision templates will guide the teams' negotiating and serve as documentation to track what is offered and countered in the session. You should provide the teams with a simple decision-making calculator so they can assess the potential impact of various offers. However, there isn't any need to build a model to assess the outcome since the teams will jointly decide if they've reached a deal and the terms of agreement. (You can build a simple model to measure the impact of that agreement, but it can be developed after the exercise.) Finally, create an agenda so everything will stay on track during the workshop.

Run: Mock negotiations typically take no more than a day to run and can be completed in half a day if they are very focused. Teams start by taking time to formulate their negotiation strategy and then meet with each other to negotiate the contract. I usually give teams time to regroup alone to discuss what they've heard, adjust their strategy, and then reengage with the other side. This is especially useful if the session involves potential negotiations with two or more partners or if there is a competitor team also trying to negotiate with the counterparty. In that case, the team representing your organization can split up to talk with the two separate counterparties. The opportunity to regroup allows the team to compare what they've heard from each of the other parties and decide what they want to ask for next before going back to talk with those teams again.

At the end of the workshop, you will need to set aside time to debrief. Start with the three questions referenced above and then discuss what was agreed upon (if anything) in the mock discussions. Debate the insights from those interactions, and agree on the next steps to take before talking with the counterparty in the real world.

Mock negotiations are also similar to lite war games for two reasons. First, if you are running a mock negotiation between your organization and one counterparty, you have the ability to stop the discussion, reverse course, and go back to try different tactics. Mock negotiations allow you to experiment and repeatedly practice particular parts of the conversation. Second, you can reconnect with the mock negotiation participants after each real-world session with the counterparty. The participants who role-played the counterparty can provide insight into the words and actions the other side took in the real talks. You can adapt your strategy and tactics before the next scheduled meeting. These ad hoc, interim meetings will build stronger negotiation capabilities in you and your group.

Premortems

Postmortems are conducted to determine why something happened in the past. For example, a pathologist conducts a postmortem on the deceased to determine the cause of death. These activities delve into the causes of an outcome that's already occurred. A premortem exercise starts with an assumption about something that will happen in the future. The analysis tries to develop what has to happen to arrive at that future outcome. For example, imagine you've traveled three years into the future and a competitor has achieved a dominant position in the market. How did they get there? What strategy did they follow? What technological or customer preferences changed? This premortem can be conducted like a war game (especially the lite version), but instead of an unknown future that is revealed through the workshop, the future state is assumed and the path(s) to get there are revealed in the session.

Design: Who are the players that could affect the assumed outcome? The existing competitors? A new competitor (this player will have to be assumed and have their role-playing fact pack built with hypothesized assets and resources)? Regulators? Distributors? What are their individual objectives? What choices can they make in the coming years to try to affect the outcome in question? And what are the rules for what can and cannot be done along the way? These questions are also asked when designing a war game workshop.

Build: Similar support materials will be needed: role-playing fact packs, an industry fact pack (including the description of what the future state is), an agenda (to keep people on track and on time), a template to keep them focused on the right choices, and a facilitator's guide (if they will be used). It's unlikely you'll need a decision-making calculator or a full model.

Run: Provide the teams with an overview of the future state, and discuss it to help everyone understand what that future world will look like. Then have the participants break out into their individual teams to develop their strategy for how they will achieve the future state. The template will help them address the same issues (with an "other" area to capture innovative thoughts). The teams then regather for a plenary discussion to share what they would do. The participants will debate which moves will survive against the choices of the others, which strategies are most likely to succeed, and the likelihood of the future state being realized.

At the end, a debrief session will pull together the collective insights. Areas to address include the following:

- What portions of the winning strategy are realistic?
- What parts of the strategy could we pursue first?
- Are there other events that could block the strategy's success?
- What remaining uncertainties must be resolved to enhance the clarity of the winning strategy?

A premortem is helpful when assessing technological changes or new regulatory policies. It can also prove useful for understanding entrepreneurs and their potential for disrupting the industry. Assign one or more teams to role-play potential entrepreneurs that could enter the market, either as new entities or invaders from another sector. These teams will be relatively unburdened by past investments and should be able to devise new ways to win.

While a premortem isn't strictly a war game, it incorporates very similar design, build, and run principles. Premortems are especially comparable to the war gaming lite construct. They are helpful for considering ways to be more innovative without falling prey to decision biases that arise in forecasting.

Two Common Business Tools That Are *Not* Competitive Exercises

There are two management techniques, often confused with war games, which have grown in popularity and use. However, they are not and won't necessarily provide the competitive insights generated from Black Hat and war gaming activities.

The first technique is gamification,[5] which broadly refers to setting up incentive mechanisms like those used in video games to encourage employees or customers to improve their performance. An example is posting customer satisfaction scores for service reps to create a contest atmosphere. The scores could be updated throughout the day, with a league table of who's winning. The software tracking the service reps' performance can also include immediate feedback and reward. The salespeople can earn more points and bonuses by consistently entering information into the tracking software. By replicating the structures that make video games so addictive (who hasn't felt time fly by while trying to make it through the next levels on Candy Crush?), gamification can improve engagement and, ultimately, performance outcomes.

While gamification is based on video games and reward mechanisms, it is not a game meant to understand competitors. I imagine it would be possible to set up an internal gamification system to reward competitive information tracking and developing competitive insight. But war game exercises are already sufficiently competitive, so adding another layer of incentives isn't necessary to draw attention to them. One of the benefits of conducting a war game is that it provides an opportunity to step out of day-to-day roles and to think strategically for a day or two. By role-playing another company, participants feel freed to think more creatively (not bound by the organization's constraints) and more aggressively (because now they can play the other side on the attack). War games don't need artificial excitement boosters—participants are already engaged throughout the day.

The second tool that isn't war gaming, but is often thought of as such, is a red team/blue team exercise. One team is assigned to be the red team, one is designated as the blue team, and they compete to see which one has the best ideas and strategies. They seldom play competing players from real life; more often, they both represent the same real-world organization. The teams might have slightly different constraints imposed upon them (say, different budgets or different access to resources), but

they rarely compete directly against each other. Instead, both are trying to beat the other by coming up with the best solution (for the same
organization).

Another common red team/blue team construct has one side arguing
"for" and the other side "against" a particular position. In a situation
like this, teams are trying to deduce the unknowns in an argument. By
taking opposite sides of the same issue, each position is stress tested.
This is clearly not a war game because the teams' choices are not interdependent with each other; they are making parallel decisions. These
exercises could help if you're weighing an acquisition decision ("Should
we buy the target, or not?"). That situation doesn't set itself up well
for a war game—unless the point of the exercise is to determine what
the next acquisition should be from among a pool of potential targets
and then the next, and the next, and so forth. A war game also helps
if you want to test how your acquisition plan performs while competing against others who are also trying to roll up the industry. In other
words, a war game can explore a merger wave in an industry to see
where all the dominos might fall. You could initiate a red team/blue
team exercise to decide if you should pay a certain amount for a particular target under consideration.

Red team/blue team exercises are closest in spirit to our Black Hat
workshops. Each of the red and blue teams wears the same black hat, but
each tries to beat the other using a better strategy for that competitor.
Recall from our previous discussion that conflicting output from each
team could lead to further confusion, so use this construct carefully.

These are examples of what some refer to more broadly as Red
Teaming.[6] If the exercise is a simulation, then it is a war game, like
we discussed above. Other common Red Team events are vulnerability
probes (seeing if the team can break the security protocols in place) or
alternative analyses (having a fresh pair of eyes review the information
and develop their own conclusion). Neither of these are strictly competitive insight exercises. They are for stress testing and often a test of
extreme uncertainties and events. These Red Team stress tests are good
for national security and resiliency to major shocks and upheavals, but
for most competitive analysis, this is not necessary and too extreme.

Ready, Set, . . . Wait

You are probably already thinking of multiple strategic questions you could tackle with these exercises, and you might even be mentally building a roster of colleagues with whom you can play these games. As much as I would love to advise you to dive in, I want to provide a bit of caution with the intent of maximizing the chance your efforts have significant impact.

When I first began to focus on war gaming, I talked with about two dozen teams who had run client war games to learn what they had done, what worked, and what they would do differently next time. I synthesized these insights with my teammates into a set of "best practices" and then started offering help to others in the firm. It took another dozen or so workshops to hone the lessons further until they felt ingrained into my mindset, though I will say I am still learning and applying new insights with each exercise I am involved in!

The primary, overarching piece of advice I can give is to "keep it simple." I don't mean make the game simplistic; rather, include only what's necessary to have a productive simulation of the real world. Only include information in the industry and role-play fact packs that's needed to make the decisions, only include decisions that are relevant for resolving the strategic uncertainty you're facing, only play the game over the timeframe that will allow you to assess the initial moves and countermoves, and only include the players that will affect you (and are affected by you). Adding extraneous information, decisions, players, or timeframes will complicate the exercise and lead to confusion among your colleagues about the true drivers of the outcomes.

If you do want to dive in and starting designing, building, and running these exercises, I suggest you start with a Black Hat or premortem focused on one competitor. These will give you the experience of pulling together the fact packs and thinking about the strategic decisions without having to wrestle with the dynamics among multiple players. A mock negotiation could also be appropriate to tackle here as long as it's a one-on-one negotiation with a supplier or customer. If you want to run a mock negotiation where you are competing against multiple different competitors to win the right to supply a third party, you should wait until you have developed your capabilities with Black Hats and premortems. Once you feel comfortable with those latter two exercises, you can move on to a lite war game, which adds in other players but doesn't require the intricacies and logistics and modeling for a traditional war game. (The multiparty mock negotiations would also be appropriate here since there is no modeling required: the team that issues the simulation's request for proposal would decide the winner.) The final hurdle to cross would be a traditional war game.

There's an old adage in the medical profession: "See one, do one, teach one." We can adapt this for competitive simulation exercises to "See, do, lead." If you're not going to build your skillset through Black Hats and then lite war games, you should instead participate in a traditional war game an expert has created for your organization. Then have someone help you while you design, build, and run traditional war games, before you are finally ready to take the lead. There is a fair bit of "art" that goes into learning the best practices, which no one could ever fully detail in a book. You may only need to "see" and "do" once before moving on to lead your own, or you may need to see and do two or three times before moving to the next stage. Ultimately, make sure your first solo venture is a success so that you earn the right to do many more in the future.

Concluding Thoughts

The most common skepticism I hear when designing and building a war game is "How can we accurately simulate what others will be doing? We can't really understand what they'll do [because they're irrational]." The text in brackets isn't always stated out loud, but it's in the subtext.

The most common feedback at the end of the exercise is "I didn't think we'd be able to replicate the competitors, but that's exactly how they'll act! That was spot on." Those helping to design and build the game felt there was no way to provide enough information to allow their colleagues to act like the competitors. However, the role-play decks did lead their fellow game participants to make choices that realistically represented how the competitor would behave. If we had missed key pieces of data or had provided the wrong guidance to the teams (e.g., asking them to pursue a different objective), their behavior in the game wouldn't have felt authentic to the others. We shouldn't be surprised. What seemed unlikely was made possible by following the process of what to collect and what questions to ask. Chapter 1's framework guides the development of role-playing fact packs. The war game's design is based on the principles of game theory, which was developed as a tool for studying how organizations will interact with each other.

Finally, remember when I said you shouldn't use war gaming for every type of decision? I'll modify that position slightly: the mindset of thinking about your competitors (and other stakeholders), their potential reactions, and the implications for your strategy *should* be ingrained in every decision you make. This mindset doesn't have to rise to the level of a traditional war game, or even a lite war game formalized event. But you should walk down the hall to your colleague who regularly wears the hat of a particular competitor and ask, "If we were to increase our prices by 5 percent in Germany, what would the competitor do?" It's pretty common in most organizations to test, probe, and determine available capabilities before executing a plan. We are in control of those processes. But the same approach to predicting how the external market will respond is not as common. Externally focused testing isn't required to be as in-depth as internal assessments, but they should be part of the analysis nonetheless. We don't actually have to switch places like Prince Edward and Tom Canty did, nor do we have to go work for the competitor for a few years before returning to our first organization. Black Hat exercises, war games (traditional and lite formats), mock negotiations, and premortems help make this analysis systematic and consistent. They'll undoubtedly become a regular part of your decision-making process.

7 Integrate Competitive Insight into the Organization

On September 11, 2001, three planes were used to attack the World Trade Center Twin Towers in New York City and the Pentagon in Washington, DC. A fourth plane was believed to have been meant to attack the US Capitol Building but failed to reach its target after the passengers on board fought the hijackers and brought it down in rural Pennsylvania. Much has been written about the 9/11 attacks, but what is relevant for our discussion comes from the 9/11 Commission report that diagnosed the errors leading up to that day.[1] In the report, the bipartisan group of former politicians and government leaders highlighted organizational challenges that contributed to a failure to foresee the attacks. While being clear they were not pointing fingers or assigning blame (given the benefit of hindsight), they nevertheless identified several key mistakes that were made.

Overall, the commission noted the following:

> The missed opportunities to thwart the 9/11 plot were also symptoms of a broader inability to adapt the way government manages problems to the new challenges of the twenty-first century. Action officers should have been able to draw on all available knowledge of al Qaeda in the government. Management should have ensured that information was shared and duties were clearly assigned across agencies, and across the foreign-domestic divide. . . . The U.S. government did not find a way of pooling intelligence and using it to guide the planning and assignment of responsibilities for joint operations involving entities as disparate as the CIA, the FBI, the State Department, the military, and the agencies involved in homeland security.[2]

One specific critique of the FBI noted that "those working counterterrorism matters did so despite limited intelligence collection and strategic analysis capabilities, a limited capacity to share information both internally and externally, insufficient training, perceived legal barriers to sharing information, and inadequate resources."[3]

One of the commission's main conclusions was that the US government had a great deal of information pointing to an imminent attack but didn't gather and share that information with the appropriate areas throughout the government. If it did, there wasn't a guarantee the attacks could have been prevented. But in prior years, the US government had foiled several plans designed to attack the country. There would have been better odds of defusing the 9/11 attacks had the knowledge within the government been shared with the appropriate parties. As the commission concluded, "The U.S. government has access to a vast amount of information. But it has a weak system for processing and using what it has. The system of 'need to know' should be replaced by a system of 'need to share.'"[4]

The challenge the US government faced at the turn of the twenty-first century is the same one facing many organizations. They have lots of information swirling around within their organization but haven't figured out a way to share it or synthesize it in an actionable way to provide meaningful insight. Recall the challenges we identified for Pepsi and their Thai operations. There were many stress points through Pepsi needing coordination in order to be best positioned to counter Sermsuk and Coca-Cola.

In this chapter, we'll examine how to create a competitive insight group within an organization. How do you integrate the competitive insight tools and frameworks so they don't conflict with the rest of the organization's operations? How does the group help support the organization's mission? How do you ensure you share what is needed with the right people in order to create an advantage for your organization?

First of all, most companies that have a function focusing on competitors call it a *competitive intelligence* function. I don't like that term because it focuses on collecting knowledge. I prefer the term *competitive insight* function because it puts the attention on implications derived from that acquired knowledge, which can be used in decision-making.[5] One of the mistakes I've observed with competitive intelligence functions is that they're solely a library function. I don't say that to denigrate librarians—having skilled talent who can efficiently access and locate the right information is extremely valuable. But the activity has to go beyond collecting data to synthesizing implications and helping the user of the information make decisions.

The competitive intelligence function at most companies is like a library: information is collected and stored, and when a business leader asks for competitor information, the competitive intelligence staff send the leader a large stack of documents. This collection of facts needs to be interpreted by the business leader, who often doesn't have time to sift through the pages and pages of material. As a result, the information isn't used, and ultimately the business leader loses faith in the competitive intelligence function.

How, then, can one create a better organizational group? There are a set of key dimensions to address, which I group into three areas: people, process, and performance. Let's start with people.

People

Best-in-class competitive insight functions require the appropriate staff. Let's break this down to highlight the key decisions.

How Many Competitive Insight Staff Members Are Needed?
In some ways this may be the most difficult question to answer because it depends on many of the answers to the subsequent questions in this chapter. However, I want to start with it because its foundational principle forms the basis for approaching all the remaining design areas.

Rule number one for a best-in-class competitive insight function is not to fight the organization. The group should seamlessly fit within the organization's structure and operate within its existing workflows. If the competitive insight function doesn't "fit" with the rest of the organization, it will be rejected either through attrition or outright hostility. This integration influences the size of the group because it needs to start small so that it doesn't become so much of a burden immediately that it's jettisoned by the rest of the organization. On the other hand, it can't be so small that it has no impact, in which case it will wither and die a slow, uneventful death. Starting with one person is definitely too few, while fifty is too many.

Where in between is the optimum? Think about how your organization is structured. If there are five business units (or divisions), then have one person track competitive insight for each division, with one person to manage the group, for six in total. Business units generally fall along geographic, product segment, brand, or customer group lines, but you should use whichever demarcation is the most important to your organization. If it's matrixed along a couple of these dimensions, then pick the one that the organization defaults to when having to prioritize. For example, if the geographic heads have solid-line reporting authority while the brand managers have dotted-line authority, then assign analysts to the geographic areas. The one thing to avoid is assigning analysts by functional area (e.g., one for operations, one for finance) since the purpose is to help business leaders make strategic decisions for your organization, not to make functional decisions.

What you don't want to do is to assign one person per major competitor. This person will have a hard time seeing across the various geographies or segments or product categories. They will focus instead on one portion of the competitor that is easiest to track. (This is similar to what we saw in chapter 1: individuals, by default, have a particular way of looking at business situations. You don't want competitors to be viewed only through marketing eyes or actions in Asia.) Find commonalities for each competitor across categories by establishing regular sessions where the five business unit analysts meet to discuss what they know about a particular competitor. Like a group of people touching various parts of an elephant, individually, they'll think they're touching different objects (e.g., snake, tree trunk, curtain). But if they talk with one another about what each has felt, they'll agree they touched the same thing. Common trends and capabilities will be uncovered by sharing insights across different divisions, geographies, or customer segments.

As the competitive insight function continues to gain traction, and develops more and better insight to improve decision-making, the group can continue to grow. The same principle applies, though: break down the analysts according to how the organization functions. If you're a group matrixed by geography and product and you initially have geographic analysts, over time you can have unique analysts tracking different product categories within a geography. For example, you might have started with a competitive insight analyst concentrating on Latin America and now want to know what the competitors are doing in health care and beauty care consumer products there. One analyst focuses on health-care products in Latin America, while another pays attention to the beauty care competitors in the region. These analysts will be able to obtain deeper insight on competitors yet still be able to develop bigger picture insights because of their periodic meetings by category (in this case, geography or product).

Start small, fitting the areas of analysis to those that are the structural foundations of the organization. Then, grow the competitive insight group over time so the analysts become more granular in scope.

What Background Should They Have?

Obviously, the analysts who staff the competitive insight group need to have exceptionally good analytic skills. They also need the ability to analyze the market along the dimensions they are assigned. If they're tracking a geography, a customer segment, or a product category, they should have some background in those areas. But as we saw in chapter 1, they need to be comfortable with uncertainty. Superforecasters do not traffic in "yes, no, or maybe." They understand the world is more nuanced and that they will never be able to reduce their predictions to such simple dimensions.

Seek analysts from inside your organization first, before hiring from the outside. Internal analyst hires will understand how the organization

operates and be better able to grease the wheels of information trans-
mission. Of course, if there are quality individuals you can add from
consulting or market research firms, by all means hire them. It can be
a great way to integrate outsiders into the organization and its culture,
helping them begin building a network within the company. Just make
sure you seek internal resources first.

The analysts also need communication and relationship-building
skills. They need to be active and assertive in connecting with the right
people in the organization. They cannot be passive participants, waiting
to receive relevant information and to be asked for insight. They'll need
to understand who *has* the information on competitors and who *needs*
the information. These are the mindsets of journalists or pollsters (constantly asking questions and willing to be rejected) and of sales people
(seeking out users of their information . . . and willing to be rejected).
The analysts have to build and maintain the connective tissue supporting the continuous flow of competitive information and insight.

Most importantly, structure these roles as temporary positions (say,
two years, max), after which the individual will transfer into a line role.
This helps keep the analysts motivated since they won't feel like they're
in a dead-end job. But it also means the future leadership will have
connections to the competitive insight function and be more likely to
use the group while progressing up the ranks. Having influencers and
champions in each of the divisions is an added benefit of cycling people through the function.

One final reminder is to build a diverse team. This was lesson 1
from the other professionals in chapter 5. Analysts with different backgrounds and perspectives will provide a more holistic view of the competitors. Those who have a marketing background will be able to better
understand the marketing signals you receive about the competitors,
and similarly with supply chain, finance, and distribution experts (to
name just a few). These areas of expertise should align with the types
of competitors' strategic moves that most challenge you to understand and predict (e.g., pricing, supply chain, market entry, product

innovation). It is especially important to create this multidimensional perspective because you're dealing with incomplete competitor data— you can't collect everything there is to know, and you can't directly ask competitors to fill in the gaps. Think of it like a jigsaw puzzle. If you gather pieces from one corner of the puzzle, you will never see the complete picture, but if you have enough pieces spread out across the puzzle, you'll be better able to visualize the complete picture.[6]

How Do You Incentivize Information Sharing?

The final people issue is establishing the right incentives across your organization. Like the US government pre-9/11, every organization I've worked with has a *lot* more competitive information inside its walls than it realizes. The problem is that the knowledge is stored inside the heads of dozens, hundreds, or thousands of employees. Sales staff hear things from customers about what competitors are offering (or asking for). Marketing team members who walk around convention floors pick up valuable insight from seeing what others are offering in their booths and from overheard conversations in the aisles. Procurement officers pick up tidbits on what competitors are asking for—and when—from discussions with suppliers. And personnel throughout the organization learn what competitors are doing by reading industry publications, attending association events, or sitting on panels with others in the industry. They take it upon themselves to gather this competitive knowledge to improve their own job performance.

Admittedly, not all of this information can be shared directly with others in your organization. Customer or supplier conversations covered by competitors' nondisclosure agreements are typically danger areas, but corporate counsel can help keep the organization safe. Recall that one of the 9/11 Commission recommendations was overcoming legal barriers to information sharing. Much of the knowledge *is* shareable, and if it were known, it would paint an insightful picture of the competitors' objectives. I know this because it's standard practice when building role-play fact packs for war game exercises! I talk with staff in the organization—even off the record—to learn what information to gather and where to obtain it as well as to establish general perceptions of how competitors behave.

But how do you systematically incentivize employees to share the knowledge in their heads? First and foremost, you must create systems that make it easier to share the information. Adding one more reporting structure will merely frustrate overworked employees, ultimately resulting in the staff ignoring the data collection. As importantly, you need to create a two-way street: the knowledge the staff shares has to be transformed into actionable insight they can act upon. Once you begin sharing useful competitive insight with the staff, they will demand more. What's the price for that? Those same employees will need to contribute even more information, creating a virtuous cycle.

Do you remember the decentralized building materials example from chapter 3? The company had a couple of large, global competitors, plus many local competitors in the dozens of countries in which they operated. They decided to maintain their competitive information collection at the country level, which was the primary structural dimension of their organization: country managers had P&L responsibility and decision-making authority. Country managers had to share the information collected with the corporate central clearing house, which would synthesize across countries and feed predictions back to each country's manager. For example, the corporate group might report, "We've seen global competitor #1 dropping prices in Laos and Thailand, so look out for them doing the same in Cambodia." When the prices actually did drop in Cambodia, the country manager was hooked. This created a virtuous cycle. The country managers found the information useful, so they shared more data in return with corporate competitive insight because they wanted more predictions. Even more information was transmitted between the countries and the corporate group, which led to more, and better, predictions. It was optimized within the normal corporate information flows.

Setting in place these systematic organizational systems is where we turn next.

Process

Having the right people in place must be complemented by the group's structure. As we've already seen, the primary rule is to make the process fit the organization, not to have one fighting with the way the organization works. Let's expand on that concept to provide a bit more clarity.

Where Should They Sit?

There are three primary areas where competitive intelligence functions are located. If the organization has a chief strategy officer (CSO), competitive intelligence will almost always be housed within their group. This is the most logical place to locate the capability, but not every organization has a CSO. There are a significant number of large companies where the CFO is responsible for strategy, while the third place where competitive intelligence functions often reside is in the marketing department.

I searched company websites for the senior executive responsible for strategy at organizations in the Fortune 1000, Fortune Global 500, and Forbes's largest privately held companies lists. I was able to identify the executive in charge of strategy for just over half of the companies, and of those, 60 percent had strategy (or strategic) in their job title, 16 percent had a financial role, and 5 percent were in the marketing department. There was some overlap and double counting (e.g., the same individual was listed as the CSO and CFO), but it still provides a great picture of who's responsible for strategy (and therefore potentially the competitive intelligence functions).[7]

I don't think there's a "bad" place to put the competitive insight group as long as it fits within a respected functional area that focuses on the organization's overall strategy. Fit is all-important! If the CSO's group only conducts business development in the form of acquisitions and due diligence, the competitive insight function will be underused. It will have much less of an impact since it won't be thinking about strategic developments within competitors—it will be seeking acquisition targets. If the CFO's group concentrates on tracking past competitor financial performance, or on M&A opportunities, the competitive insight function will also be less likely to identify strategic competitor shifts.

The rationale some companies use for placing the competitive insight group within the CMO's domain is because marketing is often tasked with finding ways to create competitive advantages. The marketing group usually tracks competitors' market share and pricing data and conducts customer surveys asking about preferences for competitors' products (often in comparison to their own company's products). Marketers know how their company stacks up against competitors because they track market data on all of them.

The problem with using these marketing efforts is the resulting knowledge isn't necessarily competitive insight. Marketing reports won't necessarily provide a sense of what new products the competitors are developing or about any future changes the competitors are planning to their pricing or marketing strategies. Are they entering new markets? That move won't show up in existing league tables. Are they thinking about acquiring others to grow their market share? Customer preferences can't provide clues to that question. In general, future strategic actions aren't evident in current or historical market data. The marketing group can be lulled into a false sense of security about their knowledge of the competition when, in fact, they have blinders on to competitors' future actions (recall the research by Montgomery, Moore, and Urbany from chapter 3).

The second potential challenge with housing the competitive insight group in the marketing department is the potential for biased thinking that the products they're selling are clearly superior to competitors' offerings. (Because they are, naturally!) They'll feel less need to rigorously assess the competition's true capabilities. If we're naturally going to beat them, why worry what they'll do? And, coupled with market data on the existing success of your products and services, there's a risk the marketing group won't be sufficiently forward-looking to anticipate competitor actions.

This isn't meant to criticize marketing departments—the same risks can occur within CFO offices. If the CFO focuses on cost efficiencies and optimizing performance, they may consider a competitor with a lower profit margin as weaker. But if that competitor is investing in marketing or R&D to enhance their product portfolio, the CFO could be missing a big future competitive threat. Regardless of where the competitive insight function is located, you need to ensure the group concentrates on understanding the future capabilities and potential actions of the competitors.

Locate the competitive insight group where it will have the most impact for your organization. It could be within the COO's domain because you're a business-to-business (B2B) company tracking competitor process innovations and shifts in supply chains. Or it could fall under the CMO's area or the CFO's group. Again, regardless of where the competitive insight function is placed within the organization, be sure they're tasked with evaluating *future* competitor moves and that they aren't lulled into looking only at existing comparative data.

Centralized or Decentralized?

Closely connected to where the group will sit is the decision to either set up the competitive insight group as a central function or to have a separate competitive insight group within each business unit. The easy answer might seem obvious: make the choice fit the organization. While the answer is true, in reality the decision is a bit more nuanced.

Most organizations have a typical structure where those in the corporate headquarters make the major decisions or push them down to the divisional level. Since competitive insight has to help decision makers with their choices, having the competitive insight group sit at the organizational level where decisions are made is the first consideration. The second is to align the group with specific types of decisions being made. Even the most centralized organization may decide to push some decisions down to middle managers. In the previous section we said you need to start gathering information for a targeted group of competitors and decisions. Align the group initially with how those decisions are made within your organization.

For example, imagine a situation where the corporate center leads in making market entry, acquisition, and customer segmentation decisions but leaves it to each division to determine optimal pricing and marketing messaging. If pricing and messaging are the initial focus of the competitive insight group, then the competitive insight analysts should sit within each division. Assign one analyst to track the competitors' pricing and another to follow their messaging. In addition, have one manager in the corporate center who oversees and coordinates the competitive insight function across divisions. The manager can also make the decision (and secure senior leadership buy-in and support) to centralize the group at the corporate center as decisions rise to those levels. As with any matrixed organization, you should create the competitive insight group to match the functional needs of the decision makers.

Let's return to the building materials company. They had a centralized group overseeing and coordinating information sharing across different geographies. However, they relied on the company's geographical structure for analysts who could talk with individual country managers in their specific purviews. Another example would be a financial services company. They had a centralized competitive insight function but organized the individual analysts around the company's different divisions, each of which had a different strategic focus (e.g., consumer, commercial, investment, global). There were one to three full-time analysts for each division, each of whom was assigned to be responsive only to that particular business unit. The analysts gathered information from the division and from secondary sources, collected and maintained the data (the basic library function), and held periodic town hall meetings and issued newsletters with synthesized insights relevant to the particular business unit. Specific personnel within each division were tasked to be collection points for the competitive insight staff, ensuring a reliable conduit of information up and down the organization. Together, division personnel and competitive insight analysts would determine if the support would be primarily reactive (the business unit requesting certain analysis) or proactive (the competitive insight function leading the way with updates and new insights). Different divisions had different needs, and the structure allowed the organization to be responsive to any of them.

The centralized group structure also allowed the full-time competitive insight analysts to regularly meet with each other. They were able to compare notes on the same competitor across different business units. If "Competitor Bank" started to make a push into the commercial business in a particular region, the information could be shared with the retail competitive insight analyst, who would then raise the issue with the retail business unit staff in that region. This structure allowed the competitive insight function to be very focused in providing detailed and relevant insights yet at the same time not lose sight of the bigger trends driving their competitors.

So, should the competitive insight group be centralized or decentralized? It depends. Make the group fit how the organization is structured and be as flexible as the organization is. Support the decision makers by integrating within their preferred decision-making processes.

What Types of Issues Should They Track?

Another critical question concerns the type of information the competitive insight group should track. Often, this will be the issue that breaks the overall initiative and leads to the competitive insight function's elimination. What seems like the obvious answer to what information is tracked is actually the wrong one. You should *not* try to gather all available information on all your competitors, nor should you try to gather whatever information is requested by any and all within the organization. Trying to be all things and all-knowing to all colleagues is impossible, especially in the initial stages of setting up the competitive insight group. Instead, start small and be focused.

This seems counterintuitive. It will inevitably lead to situations where someone in the organization asks the competitive insight group for help with a particular topic or particular competitor, only to be told,

"Sorry, we can't help you with that right now." The idea of turning away a potential user, and the fear that this will create insurmountably negative perceptions within the organization, is anathema to anyone well versed in customer service. However, accepting the request risks providing information that carries no actionable insight—especially if the information is needed quickly and the competitive insight analyst has to produce something from scratch. The recipient will almost certainly view the competitive insight group as worthless. Recall the advice from the NICU nurse at the end of lesson 3: sometimes it's best to *not* perform a test if you know that waiting will provide a superior answer.

Instead, the competitive insight group should respond, "Unfortunately, we don't currently track that competitor [or that topic], but we'll make note of it and add it to the list of areas to address in the future. In the meantime, we can offer insight into how another comparable competitor is addressing a similar issue, and we'd be happy to set up time to discuss with you how to apply this information to your situation." Every strategist worth her salt will tell you that developing a good strategy includes being explicit about what you will do as well as what you will *not* do. The same should be true for your competitive insight function. (And let's be honest, if the employee requesting the competitive insight is persistent and has enough seniority, she may be able to convince others to expand the competitive insight group.)

Start small and select one or two competitors to track. Ask several key strategic decision makers which competitors they'd like to know more about. Ask those leaders which kinds of choices they've found the most challenging to make, for example, pricing, market entry, product portfolio, acquisitions, or partnerships. Choose a subset of their answers, and get the competitive insight group up to speed quickly on the specific competitors and insight requested. This will lead to immediate, practical insight. Once those competitors and situations are understood and monitored going forward (by setting the right metrics to track, at the right intervals), then expand the effort to additional competitors or decision choices. Start small, stay focused, and earn the right to build more capability by delivering on the group's promises.

How Should You Collect the Information?

We saw in the people section that you need to incentivize individuals in your organization to share information with the competitive insight function. Begin by using existing reporting processes and start by adding a small number of questions that gather competitive intelligence. As the process becomes more ingrained, the amount collected can increase.

For example, in the customer relationship management (CRM) system the sales force uses, add two additional items to the postincident form. The first is a multiple-choice question: "which competitors came up in your conversation today?" Follow this by the top three (at most) important competitors to track (identified above), with a fourth box for "other" and a text entry option. The second item would be "which topics came up in conversation related to the competitors?" Follow this by the set of topics the group wants to cover (identified above): pricing, product introduction, market entry, and so on with an "other" box and text entry option. If you want to push the sales force, you can also add a "Check here if you want to speak with someone in the competitive insight function about something you've heard." That will be more likely to lead to thoughtful information than having the sales agent type in a long answer to a free text box.

Admittedly, this data won't provide immediate insight into the competitors' plans, but it accomplishes two things. First, it starts training the sales force to be thinking about competitors and noting when they come up in sales discussions. (It may even push a few to ask questions aimed at learning more about competitors' offerings or pricing. Remember to have in-house counsel set rules for what can be asked.) The second is that it provides a simple awareness tracker for which competitors are being talked about and with regard to which topics. It is very easy to create a simple algorithm that tracks the number of mentions of each competitor and the frequency with which topics arise. If multiple competitors were indicated on the CRM form, the system won't tell you which ones were mentioned in conjunction with which topic, but if the output starts showing multiple competitors and multiple topics across sales agents, that's a good indicator that competitors are pushing hard (like we discussed in chapter 4). The competitive insight function staff will also now be in a much better position to follow up with the sales force to ask targeted questions: "You indicated that you've heard about Competitor X from all your accounts this week, and all with regard to pricing. Can we talk with you for ten minutes about what you've been hearing?"

The same process should be followed with the reporting mechanisms used by other frontline staff. When the procurement office talks with their suppliers, or logistics talks with distributors, have them record the same simple information. You can also add to existing after-action reports for when R&D staff attend conferences or when anyone in the organization attends an industry convention.

As the competitive insight function and process gets more ingrained within the organization, you can slowly add more questions and more multiple-choice options to the various systems, with more open-ended response opportunities. It should never get overwhelming for the front-line staff—add one question at a time, and after it's been used for several weeks, ask them whether they've noticed the new question and for their feedback on how to make it easier to use.

When Should the Competitive Insight Group Be Used?

You've set up the right format, you have the right people in place, and you've determined the types of competitive insight they'll focus on first. The final issue to address is when to require the group's use in strategic decision-making. Should you even require it at all, opting instead for an organic internal knowledge market to develop? As an economist, I might naturally default to answering, "Let the market decide." However, in this case, I think there's a bit of nudging needed to seed the internal market and create a good foundation upon which it can grow.[8] What would these prescribed competitive insight mandates look like?

One option would be to require the competitive insight function be used before any C-suite strategic presentation. As an example, the CEO of the financial services company described above would ask at the outset of every strategic meeting, "Did you vet this with the competitive insight group?" If the answer was "no," the project leader had to immediately leave the session, meet with the competitive insight function in the coming days to discuss the idea, and then reschedule their presentation. As expected, this didn't happen very often. The CEO did not mandate that the presenter change their proposal or adhere to the competitive insight function's recommendations, but it created a subtle enforcement mechanism and a norm that the competitive insight function was a valued sounding board to vet the ideas and incorporate different perspectives.

Moreover, the CEO knew the ideas had been tested against the expected market response. Middle managers often believe their organization is superior to competitors, and therefore they dismiss competitor products and services as inferior. The competitive insight function can act as a devil's advocate and independent voice to highlight the ways in which competitors would attack the new bread slicer idea. Remember the advice from the detective and paleontologists in lesson 8. Having someone play the role of devil's advocate can help prevent you from getting locked into one way of viewing the world.

A second way to nudge the use of the competitive insight group is to require senior leaders to set aside 10 to 25 percent of each monthly/quarterly/annual strategy meeting to discuss the industry's evolution. The twist, however, is each participant would be assigned to debate the topics from a different competitor's or stakeholder's perspective. The participants will have to work with the competitive insight function to ensure they understand their assigned role and can speak to the topics wearing their role-play hat. Participants should maintain the same role-play assignment for several cycles so they can build up familiarity and competency with that competitor. Switch roles periodically to keep the exercise fresh. (This strategy meeting exercise is an application of ongoing war gaming lite concepts.)

Even though you can start this process with a more formalized war game or Black Hat exercise to develop the initial competitor insight, you don't need to go to that extreme. Use the guidance in chapters 1 and 6 to develop the initial role-play fact packs. As described earlier, assign each senior leader one organization to track in the coming months, which will require them to maintain up-to-date information and insight on the competitor/stakeholder they role-play. The leaders will have to work with their direct reports and the competitive insight function to collect and synthesize the information. This creates an extra advantage of building an immediate relationship between the business units and the competitive insight group.

This second approach spreads the responsibility for tracking competitors among the senior leaders. Instead of having to track three to six key competitors, each executive only has to track one. The other leaders will know who to talk with to get insight on other competitors if the need arises between quarterly meetings.

Having these regular role-play meetings to discuss the latest industry developments will help uncover which competitors feel most threatened or most advantaged (which will inform the chapter 4 analysis). The disciplined effort also identifies which competitors the organization should study further to hone their competitive insight (our frameworks in chapters 1 and 2). It will be less likely that a competitor will avoid your attention and shock the company. The leadership will be concentrating on the competition: who is strong, who feels they are weak, and who don't we know enough about? Possible starter topics for these regular meetings include

1. current news and developments in the industry (e.g., new products, acquisitions, pricing changes, leadership movement),
2. potential strategic challenges the organization faces, and
3. longer-term changes in the industry (e.g., regulatory shifts, geopolitical developments, scientific/technological innovations, customer trends).

Ad hoc discussions held between regular senior leadership meetings will also provide an opportunity to slip on the competitors' hats and push the strategic thinking. As a plan develops, leaders can ask for a short discussion: "Put on your competitor hat, and tell us how you'd react to our plan." By debating the industry dynamics and evolution wearing competitor role-play hats, the executives will be less likely to fall into the trap of assuming the industry will evolve (and competitors will make choices) in a way that benefits the organization's preferred outcome.

Performance

As with any organizational change, you'll need to follow up on the implemented competitive insight processes to track how well they're helping to improve the company's performance. I'll discuss some metrics you can use to assess how well the competitive insight group is doing and then explore a related issue of how to excite senior leadership about the need for a competitive insight function.

How to Measure Competitive Insight Performance

As with any organization, the metrics used to assess the competitive insight group's performance should be related to the objectives the company wants to pursue. Let's suppose a company is trying to increase market share. They can measure the change in their market share relative to a competitor's market share instead of simply tracking their own change. Numbers greater than one are desirable. Below are a few suggested metrics to think about using, but they should be adapted to the organization's specific needs.

Internal metrics fall into three categories: individual, group, and corporate. For each individual in the competitive insight function, you could measure

- satisfaction surveys from the business unit and C-suite personnel the competitive insight analyst works with,
- how accurate the analyst's predictions were,
- the growth in the number of staff who have competitive insight knowledge, and

- the growth in the number of staff from whom competitive information is gathered.

For the group, you can use metrics similar to the ones above but aggregated across the entire competitive insight function. You can also measure

- the percentage of senior-level reports on which the competitive insight group signed off, and
- the revenue (and growth in revenue) of all products the competitive insight function interacted with (remember, you'll be starting small, so this will demonstrate how much and how fast the competitive insight group is affecting all areas of the business).

Finally, corporate-level performance should be measured relative to (tracked) competitors' performance. Metrics could include

- earnings per share (EPS) growth relative to competitor EPS,
- market share (and growth) relative to competitors,
- profit (and growth) relative to competitors (using whichever profit measure, e.g., EBIT, EBITDA, net income, is most relevant for the industry), and
- new product introductions relative to the competitors'.

Metrics like these will help assess whether the competitive insight function is serving the organization's needs and creating a positive, growing impact on the company's performance overall.

How to Secure Senior Leadership Buy-In

It's important to have senior leadership support for the initiative because competitive insight functions are typically seen as cost centers. They don't sell any products or services in the external market and therefore don't directly generate any revenue. Without senior leadership support, the competitive insight group will almost certainly be on the chopping block the next time the company needs to cut costs. Having a robust set of measurements, like those detailed above, will help prove the group's impact.

But the question really is how you can convince senior leadership in the first place that a competitive insight function is needed, before you have sufficient internal data to make the case? To drum up support, start by collecting stories about a time when the company faced a harsh competitive response. Gather these anecdotes by talking to various managers from different divisions and regions. Ask them to describe situations when they were surprised by a competitor's move or when they had a brilliant new idea but a competitor's action nullified the expected gains. Once you have sufficient tales from around the organization (and the bigger the competitive effect, the better), develop a narrative showing how the competitive insight function, and the frameworks from chapters 1 through 4, could have allowed you to predict the competitor's response before it happened.

Sure, you can't *prove* that the hindsight knowledge would have been perfectly predictive. But you're not trying to prove the fact. You're trying to spur the senior executives to share "horror stories" with each other. A hypothetical example of such a tale could be as follows:

> Remember when our primary multinational competitor drastically lowered their prices in Africa, right when we launched our new product? And how that led to a $100 million write-off? Remember how we keep saying, 'If only we knew, we'd have been able to survive that attack?' We now realize they did the same thing to two of our other competitors in Europe and Asia when they both tried to launch a new product. We didn't notice at the time we entered Africa because those European and Asian products never took off. But we should have known—and could have known! We need a competitive insight function so it doesn't happen again. $100 million surprises should not be the norm.

Once you have initial support to begin the group, immediately start collecting performance metrics like those highlighted above. In particular, make predictions, track their success, and measure the impact on the business. This data will be justification for the competitive insight function enduring. Follow up occasionally with line managers after providing them with predictions. Ask them, "How much would we have lost if you hadn't been ready for the competitor's response?" Again, the questions aren't meant to create proof-beyond-a-reasonable-doubt counterfactuals. The answers will create a narrative that the competitive insight function is making a difference.

Many competitive insight functions wither and die because they're an easy target for cost cutting in times of need. But with really good stories and supporting metrics, the organization will be better able to see the value being created. Leadership will continue to invest and grow the capability.

Competitive Insight Dashboard

Organizations have implemented multiple dashboards to help track the voluminous "big data" swirling around from inside and outside their walls. Marketing dashboards track consumer sentiment and pricing, while operations dashboards track inventory levels and supplier pricing. And other dashboards keep track of financial metrics. However, while it's crucially important to track competitive data, I have yet to find a dashboard that tracks and addresses the type of data and competitive information outlined in this book.

There are a few that will track historical information on competitors' pricing, patents, market share, and publicly available financial data, but remember that these are the competitors' outcomes, not the drivers of the choices they will make in the future. A comprehensive dashboard would track the historical metrics as well as text-mined trends in the words included in the competitor's press releases and public documents. This is step 1 in chapter 1. The dashboard should also track information on competitors' capacity, partnerships, R&D spending, job postings, and brand value—chapter 1, step 2. These are the drivers of future assets and resources, not just existing ones. The dashboard should also track new hires and include their backgrounds (chapter 1, step 3). Remember lesson 3 from chapter 5: be systematic when collecting data so it's available when needed.

But most critically, the dashboard should also be a place to prompt the user to enter predictions. It should store those predictions and tag elements of the dashboard used to inform them so when those dashboard elements are updated, the user is prompted to review the prediction. It would also have an end date to the prediction (remember, this is best practice from chapter 1 and *Superforecasting*; have short-term predictions with a definitive conclusion). When that date occurs, the system would prompt the user to assess whether the prediction came true or not (allowing for some ambiguity, especially for predictions about the competitor's internal processes, which are hard to know with certainty from the outside).

You may be thinking, "that sounds pretty cool . . . how can we get it?" I wish I could offer you a link to it. Unfortunately, the biggest challenge is not the structure of the dashboard but aggregating the data.[9] The historical market-level data exists and can be imported into a system (as it is for most business analytic dashboards), but remember, the data we want is the competitor-specific information on the drivers of future choices. It exists on the competitor websites, but it's not stored in the same place for each organization. Currently, it would take too much time and manual effort to set up all the links to each competitor's individual web pages with the relevant information for the dashboard to be in a position to scrape the data. Of course, those links could all be broken the following week if the competitor updated their website. (It's happened to me—I compiled the URLs for the executive management biographies at Fortune 1000/Global 500 firms, and when I went back a few weeks later to see if there was a change in leadership, some of the links had already been broken.) The other challenge is that when the data is compiled all in one external place (like executives' backgrounds on LinkedIn), there are limits to scraping those sites.

Begin developing a competitive insight dashboard by using the market analytics dashboard your organization already uses, but realize it's not sufficient. You need to supplement it with information on the drivers of future decisions, and unfortunately ML hasn't developed to the point where you can instruct a bot to go surf the competitors' websites for the information you seek. Ask your organization's IT department if they can create a simple interface to import the after-action feedback sourced above (in the "How Should You Collect the Information?"

section), plus a place for the competitive insight staff to manually enter notes on competitors with a simple tagging function. Use it as a place to store the data so it will be easier to search (remember the NICU nurses' use of digitized health charts in lesson 7 from chapter 5), and eventually begin building the AI/ML analytics to mine it for further insights.

Everyone thinks they understand what competitive intelligence is, but most people don't. It isn't just reading about competitors. It's pulling together data from multiple sources and triangulating an independent estimate of likely behavior. As the competitive insight leader at the financial services company told me, he often found the competitive intelligence work of others to be full of holes: "Most companies view competitive intelligence as information, not insight." The latter is the key.

I know it's unlikely I'll persuade every organization to change the name of their competitive intelligence function to "competitive insight function." But even without a name change, think about structuring the group within your organization as one not only collecting information but also synthesizing it into usable insights to help drive strategic decisions. Integrate it seamlessly so everyone feels a need to share their competitive knowledge with others throughout the organization. You don't have to create as many new entities as the US government did in reaction to the 9/11 attacks or ones that are as large. Start small and earn the right to grow as you demonstrate the effectiveness.

IV Conclusion

Copyright © M

8   You *Can* Understand Your Competitor

Why do we need to worry about competitors? Haven't businesses, markets, and the economy changed in the digital age, so platforms and consumer-centric strategies are all that's required? I would argue competitive principles still apply and are timeless. We live in a world of finite resources, and there are always other groups working to increase their share of those resources. One of the most basic concepts of business strategy is determining how to create value and how to capture that value. Creating value is where platforms, partnerships, joint ventures, and consumer-centric concepts really flourish. But capturing value is still a contest, one between you and your platform partners, between your organization and downstream suppliers, and even one between you and your customers. My hope is this book will help you better understand the mindset of those with whom you interact so you can capture more value for your organization. If that entails creating more value for your platform or other ecosystem stakeholders to capture than they would have otherwise, so be it!

Competitors are not irrational. Ancient Greek philosophers used "rational" to refer to those who use facts and reason (i.e., a logical, structured analysis) to learn about the world. The rational individual was differentiated from those who rely on sensory experience ("I saw it!") or divine or institutional authority as the source of knowledge. In other words, if we rely on facts and evaluate them using a systematic and consistent method of analysis, we are being rational. Competitors seem to be irrational because we project our goals and objectives onto them. Or we want them to make choices that will help us achieve our goals even if we don't consciously admit this to ourselves.

Competitors are truly irrational when they make choices that don't help achieve *their* objectives or when they make random choices that aren't supported by the fact base *they* face. It's possible that large competitors against whom you regularly compete are irrational, but it would also mean they became as successful as they are by pure luck. We know that's highly unlikely. Instead, we should assume they are rational; we just haven't figured out their objectives yet. And we haven't looked at the competitive landscape from their perspective. If we do, their rationality becomes clearer.

I genuinely hope the frameworks and processes outlined in this book will provide a foundation upon which to build your competitive insight capabilities. From the basic framework in chapter 1 about "getting inside your competitor's head" to the more targeted sets of questions helping predict how they'll react to you and how they'll move spontaneously, you now have a simple set of structured analyses that are repeatable across competitors and across time. From the tips and tricks we can learn from other professionals who cannot ask directly for clarification from the subjects of their research and care and investigation, you now have some additional ways to adjust your mindset to be more systematic in your approach. Finally, you have a set of exercises and workshops you can conduct with others in your company, plus guidance on how to embed these processes throughout your organization.

I want to encourage you to consider the advice in this book as first principles. They are the basis upon which any competitive strategy can be built. I have often found common strategic advice hard to apply. I understand why you might want to shift to a portion of the market where there is little competition. But what if a competitor (or more than one) follows you there? Or what if there is no competition because other companies have tried and failed to succeed in that space? What if all the competitors decide to invade that new space (because they've heard the same advice), which would have left you alone in the original market?

There is never a checklist that says "Here are the specific conditions that need to be true in the industry and your organization for this strategic move to be the right answer." They are a set of potential tools, but the strategist must determine what's right. The generic advice feels like the theoretical game theory solutions we talked about. Strategic advisors lay out an understanding of the competitor but often revert to focusing on you and what you should do, without returning to thinking about the competitors' reactions to you. It's not the main focus of the strategic advice; I want to put the focus on the competitor and thinking about how you play the (continual) game against them as front and center. This book's goal is to help put you in the proper mindset vis-à-vis your competitors and others in the ecosystem (e.g., platform partners, suppliers, distributors, complementors, and any other group with whom you have interdependent engagement) so you can determine which of those strategic levers are the right ones to pull. If you can define the game you are playing, I have the utmost confidence you can find the right solution. Remember, competitive insight is a mindset, not a tool.

There is one final exercise I'd like to leave you with. It's a modification of one I use to help companies identify their competitive advantage. Pick a competitor (one you regularly confront in the marketplace), and write down what you think is distinctive about them. What makes them better than you? What factors make customers choose their product or service? What are the capabilities and competencies they possess that you and others don't?

Now review the list. Could a customer or supplier look at it and think that it described you instead of the competitor? If so, you haven't figured out the differences between you and them. Yes, some competitors behave like you do, but there's always something different about them. Your job is to figure out what that "something" is. Once you do, you'll be better able to predict what they can do differently from you, which is where the real threats to your strategic plans lie.

I started this conclusion by arguing that competitors still matter—that we're still competing with others in an attempt to capture value in the market. However, I would also point out again that these frameworks, processes, and mindsets—and therefore the insights—can also be applied to others in your broader market or network. For example, you can assess how suppliers or distributors will react to your strategic plans. How will platform complementors use your platform to enhance their own offerings? Are significant customers contemplating switching their processes, eliminating the need for your products and services (or increasing the possibility a competitor will enter the fray to compete for the contract)? Governmental changes can lead to shifts in regulations and policy, and geopolitical actors are often deemed "irrational" when they make choices that we would not make (or want them to make). Globalization has been under attack the last few years, but it will still be a fundamental part of managing business in the future, so use these techniques to try and understand the political tea leaves too.

Chapter 1's framework can be used to think about what those changes might be—regardless of who the other organization is. It's true you don't face the constraint of being unable to talk directly with these other stakeholders. But if you've ever left a meeting with any of them thinking, "I'm not quite sure we got the whole story there," use the concepts and frameworks in this book to gain better insight into their mindset. If the analysis confirms what they said, you will have comforting reassurance. But if their statements and your insights tell different stories, the dissonance provides you the knowledge and ability to dig deeper in subsequent conversations, probing until you uncover their true intent.

At their core, the frameworks and techniques described in this book are designed to make you more empathetic to those within your broader ecosystem regardless of what your organization does or how other groups interact with you. We've focused on competitors, but the same principles apply to partners, complementors, and anyone else with whom you interact. They likewise apply to business situations, governmental interactions (local, national, and international), and charitable organizations.

Walk a mile in the shoes of others. Look at the world from their perspective. They're trying to survive and thrive just like you are. If you can adopt their mindset and understand why they do what they do, you'll be in a much better position to make the best choices to help yourself succeed. And that's the ultimate goal.

Acknowledgments

Whenever I've read the acknowledgments in a book, I'm always amazed at how many people get thanked. I wondered if that many individuals really contributed to the book's production. Having now gone through the process, I can confirm that many people have a role to play in the journey from idea to publication. I would like to add my contribution to that tradition.

The first people I need to thank are my family members. My wife Maggie and my three sons have been very supportive throughout the process. They encouraged me to keep working when I would get discouraged. One of my sons would admonish me that I needed to keep working so I wouldn't miss the publisher's deadline! My youngest, who still dreams of becoming a paleontologist, helped me draft the introduction to chapter 5.

Thanks to two of my economics professors as an undergraduate at the University of Michigan: Ken Binmore taught me game theory and instilled a love for, and wonderment about, the subject; and Jim Adams encouraged me to apply to PhD programs in economics and supported me along the way. I also must thank Eric Maskin, who taught me game theory in the PhD program at Harvard, for making me believe I could understand the topic at a more rigorous level.

Many people helped me while I was at McKinsey & Company. Lenny Mendonca was a believer in me from the first day and continually encouraged me to pursue dreams (like writing a book). Janamitra Devan gave me the runway to become a war gaming expert. John Stoner is the living embodiment of a supportive mentor. He was the partner on one of the first war games I designed, built, and ran. He also gave me my first opportunity to lead a client war gaming project because "you know what you're doing." Kevin Coyne stepped in to lead our team when we were struggling and provided more opportunities than I had ever dreamed were possible. Hugh Courtney helped me understand the game theory workshops he ran for clients, allowing me to build upon them with war gaming, and Andrew Sellgren helped me with the transition into the firm, where I stepped into the shoes Hugh and Andrew had previously filled. Tom Herbig inspired the idea behind chapter 5 ("what if we ask homicide detectives how they do their job since they can't talk to the dead body?"). Jayanti Kar and Devesh Mittal were valuable teammates when I started and helped me as I learned the ropes. Renee Dye was a great sounding board to keep me centered and encouraged me to believe in myself and my abilities. Bill Wiseman gave me confidence by sending me in his place to meet with the chairperson of our large high-tech client because "you are the war gaming expert." Kevin McLellan and Melissa Sueling welcomed me into their pricing practice efforts to run multiple mock negotiations. Allen Webb was always willing to listen to article ideas I had and helped push several through to fruition. Sean Brown provided a valuable connection after I left the firm and began working on this book. And I thank the others too numerous to mention, including those in the strategy practice, which was my home for nine years.

I would also be remiss if I didn't thank all the clients I've been fortunate enough to work with on war gaming and competitive dynamics over the years. I obviously can't name any of them, but their willingness to trust me with the big, messy strategic questions provided all the fodder for developing the ideas that appear in this book.

This book is also a synthesis of, and expansion on, articles, research, and discussions with numerous coauthors. I had many deep conversations, writing sessions, and redrafts with Dan Lovallo, Hugh Courtney, Jayanti Kar, Kevin Coyne, and Marla Capozzi.

There are a few people I need to call out at the Olin Business School at Washington University in St. Louis. Mahendra Gupta took a chance on turning a consultant into a professor. Anne Marie Knott has been supportive of my ideas and was the connection to my agent (without whom this book wouldn't have been published). Peter Boumgarden has been willing to debate these ideas with me, especially delving into the philosophical question of what it means to be rational. Todd Milbourn has provided moral support and friendship in all my efforts. Thanks to Mark Taylor and Ohad Kadan for their support and trust in what I can contribute, and to the members of the economics department at Olin for providing me with a welcome home. Finally, thanks to all the students I've had the privilege of teaching, especially those who listened to me expound on the ideas that appear in this book. One of those former students, Kevin Farr, and his partner at CNTRD, Michael Hsiung, were instrumental in helping me brainstorm the possibilities for a competitive insight dashboard.

I wish I could thank by name the interviewees who volunteered their time to discuss their analytic processes that turned into chapter 5. I am eternally grateful for their willingness to share their time with someone outside of their field and to self-reflectively discuss their own experiences and ideas.

Special thanks to Esmond Harmsworth, my agent at Aevitas. He showed faith in my ability to complete this book and worked harder than I expected to help me format a successful proposal. He kept pushing me to refine my thinking and bring clarity to my arguments, which has resulted in a better book than I had envisioned.

Thank you to Emily Taber, Kathleen Caruso, Antonn Park, and the staff at the MIT Press. Emily's comments and feedback on the early drafts also helped shape the book into a much better version of what I had always intended it to be. Kathleen and Antonn helped polish the book into its finished state. I am also thankful for the feedback from three anonymous reviewers. Their comments forced me to think about how to present the ideas in a clearer fashion. I am honored to be part of this new series and part of the MIT family.

Thanks to Amanda DeBord, who edited an early draft of the book. The cleaner version she framed helped me focus on the concepts as I was finishing the draft.

Finally, there are too many friends and family members to thank who have supported me along the way. I would like to thank my mother, Noël Horn, for her love and help editing my first draft of this book. To my sister Jackie Horn and brother Chris Horn, who played games with me while growing up, including many we invented ourselves; they helped me start down this gaming path. Special thanks to Candice and Andy Clauss, Stevie and Margaux Drake, Greg and Sarah Jane Eastman, Steve and Lindsay Kafka, and Paul and Elaine O'Connell for years of support. And finally, thanks to my aunt and uncle, Tim and Leslie Worcester, for constant encouragement and support throughout the years.

Notes

Introduction

1. Tyler Clifford, "Domino's Pizza CEO Says There Is 'Irrational Pricing' in the Rival Third-Party Delivery Marketplace," CNBC, October 8, 2019, https://www.cnbc.com/2019/10/08/dominos-ceo-irrational-pricing-exists-in-the-delivery-marketplace.html.

2. Since the survey was conducted in English, it was distributed to individuals at the director level and above in businesses in the United States, Canada, the United Kingdom, and India.

3. This excludes all "don't know" survey responses within each strategic category.

4. The irrationality questions and the surprised questions were on different screens during the survey. It's unlikely the participants remembered all thirteen answers in the exact order and repeated them, and it's also unlikely they went back and wrote down the answers to the irrationality question. It's reasonable to assume these were independent answers.

5. Throughout the book, if I use a company's name, then I have not had a consulting relationship with them (at least on the issues that I have written about). Any example with company names comes from outside-in analysis and secondary sources. Companies that I have consulted with are referred to by anonymous names or with reference to their industry.

6. "Branson Challenges BSkyB over ITV," *BBC News*, November 19, 2006, http://news.bbc.co.uk/2/hi/business/6163162.stm.

7. Fergus Sheppard, "BSkyB's ITV Move under Fire," *The Scotsman*, November 21, 2006.

8. Lisa Murray, "Murdoch Slams Broadband and Crowe Film," *Sydney Morning Herald*, November 16, 2006.

9. https://twitter.com/elonmusk/status/873116351316938753.

10. Dan Ariely, a prominent behavioral economist, has argued that even if these traits are irrational (from the theoretical point of view), they are so consistent across decision makers that they are predictable. This is the key we'll be focusing on: if your competitor's actions are consistent and explainable, they are predictable. See Dan Ariely, *Predictably Irrational: The Hidden Forces That Shape Our Decisions* (New York: HarperCollins, 2008).

Chapter 1

1. This framework is based on Hugh Courtney, John Horn, and Jayanti Kar, "Getting into Your Competitor's Head," *McKinsey Quarterly*, no. 1 (April 2009): 128–137. It builds upon work by others such as Michael E. Porter, *Competitive Strategy* (New York: The Free Press, 1980), 47–74; Michael Porter, "Analyzing Competitors: Predicting Competitor Behavior and Formulating Offensive and Defensive Strategy," in *Policy, Strategy, & Implementation: Readings and Cases*, ed. Milton Leoniades (New York: Random House Business Division, 1983), 192–209; and Leonard M. Fuld, *The Secret Language of Competitive Intelligence* (New York: Crown Business, 2006).

2. This is based on a case on Boston Consulting Group's interview preparation website: https://careers.bcg.com/case-interview-preparation (accessed March 23, 2022).

3. Philip E. Tetlock and Dan Gardner, *Superforecasting: The Art and Science of Prediction* (New York: Broadway Books, 2015).

4. Prediction markets allow individuals to buy and sell $1 shares of a certain statement being true. For example, "Ford will sell 15,000 electric vehicles in the next six months." The shares are traded and have a price between $0 and $1. If the price was $0.60 and you thought the probability of the statement being true was 65 percent, you'd buy the share, driving up the price. Prediction markets are a way of aggregating multiple perspectives to get an efficient group estimate in certain circumstances. See James Surowiecki, *The Wisdom of the Crowds: Why the Many Are Smarter Than the Few and How Collective Wisdom Shapes Business, Economies, Societies and Nations* (New York: Doubleday, 2004).

5. The appendix of *Superforecasting* has additional guidance on how to improve prediction performance.

6. Chris Mulligan, Nicholas Northcote, Tido Röder, and Sasha Vesuvala, "The Strategy-Analytics Revolution," *McKinsey Quarterly* (April 26, 2021).

7. As ML continues to develop, it's possible that future models could be able to both contemplate discontinuous moves based off previous choices in the model as well as update the likelihood of certain moves dependent on what has occurred in the simulation. This latter updating can already be done to increase the likelihood of responses being taken in the future because they have been taken more often in the past, but what the models must do is to update the likelihood of *new* choices being made based on the changes in the prior moves in the model.

8. Daniel Goleman, "Hot to Help: When Can Empathy Move Us to Action?," *Greater Good Magazine*, March 1, 2008, https://greatergood.berkeley.edu/article /item/hot_to_help (accessed May 15, 2020).

9. Marco Iacoboni, *Mirroring People: The New Science of How We Connect with Others* (New York: Farrar, Straus, and Giroux, 2008).

10. Jeremy Hogeveen, Michael Inzlicht, and Sukhvinder S. Obhi, "Power Changes How the Brain Responds to Others," *Journal of Experimental Psychology: General* 143, no. 2 (April 2014): 755–762.

Chapter 2

1. http://us.pg.com/who-we-are/structure-governance/corporate-structure (accessed March 23, 2022).

2. https://us.pg.com/annualreport2021/our-integrated-strategy-to-win/ (accessed March 23, 2022).

3. Pepsi has been in Thailand since 1953 (https://www.suntorypepsico.co.th /brandDetail.html?id=1; accessed March 27, 2022), while Coca-Cola has been there since 1949 (https://connect.amchamthailand.com/list/member/coca-cola -thailand-limited-1310; accessed March 27, 2022).

4. https://www.forbes.com/largest-private-companies/list/ (accessed March 14, 2022).

Chapter 3

1. This chapter is based on Kevin Coyne and John Horn, "Predicting Your Competitor's Move," *Harvard Business Review* (April 2009).

2. David B. Montgomery, Marian Chapman Moore, and Joel E. Urbany, "Reasoning about Competitive Reactions: Evidence from Executives," *Marketing Science* 24, no. 1 (Winter 2005): 138–149.

3. Steven B. Most, Daniel J. Simons, Brian J. Scholl, Rachel Jimenez, Erin Clifford, and Christopher F. Chabris, "How Not to Be Seen: The Contribution of Similarity and Selective Ignoring to Sustained Inattentional Blindness," *Psychological Science* 12, no. 1 (January 2001): 9–17.

4. Kevin Coyne and John Horn, "How Companies Respond to Competitors: A McKinsey Global Survey," *McKinsey Quarterly* (April 2008).

5. We chose the same category of strategic decisions as Montgomery, Moore, and Urbany. These are also competitor choices that should be easy to observe since they are executed in the marketplace (as opposed to talent management or R&D, which are internally focused within a competitor).

6. The survey found that about 20 percent of respondents didn't know how many options they considered, so it's possible that these are lower bounds.

Chapter 4

1. Kevin Coyne and John Horn, "How Companies Can Understand Competitors Moves: A McKinsey Global Survey," *McKinsey Quarterly* (December 2008).

2. Peter Boumgarden, Jackson Nickerson, and Todd Zenger, "Sailing into the Wind: Exploring the Relationships between Ambidexterity, Vacillation, and Organizational Performance," *Strategic Management Journal* 33, no. 6 (June 2012): 587–610.

3. Josh Bersin, "What to Expect from Leadership Changes at the Top," *Entrepreneur*, October 24, 2017.

4. Ayse Karaevli and Edward J. Zajac, "When Is an Outsider CEO a Good Choice?," *MIT Sloan Management Review*, June 19, 2012.

5. The Conference Board, "CEO Succession Practices in the Russell 3000 and S&P 500: 2021 Edition," June 21, 2021.

6. This is referred to as self-serving bias.

7. For example, Henry Mintzberg, *The Rise and Fall of Strategic Planning* (New York: The Free Press, 1994); and Michael Allison and Jude Kaye, *Strategic Planning for Nonprofit Organizations: A Practical Guide for Dynamic Times* (Hoboken, NJ: John Wiley & Sons, 2015).

8. Steve Case, *The Third Wave: An Entrepreneur's Vision of the Future* (New York: Simon & Schuster, 2016), 56.

9. William Foster-Harris, *The Basic Patterns of Plot* (Norman: University of Oklahoma Press).

10. Christopher Booker, *Seven Basic Plots: Why We Tell Stories* (London: Bloomsbury Continuum).

11. Mike Figgis, *The Thirty-Six Dramatic Situations* (London: Faber & Faber), which is an updated version of Georges Polti's original list from the nineteenth century.

Chapter 5

1. All the experts who spoke with me were guaranteed anonymity. There were twelve paleontologists, ten archaeologists, three NICU nurses, and one (retired) homicide detective. I could not get any police departments to allow me to speak with their detectives, and it was hard to secure time with the NICU nurses—but I didn't push too hard because of the stress all health-care workers have felt during COVID.

2. Michael E. Porter, "What Is Strategy?," *Harvard Business Review* (November–December 1996).

Chapter 6

1. Geoff Colvin, *Talent Is Overrated: What Really Separates World-Class Performers from Everybody Else* (New York: Portfolio, 2008).

2. Bain & Company, "Management Tools & Trends," https://www.bain.com/insights/topics/management-tools-and-trends (accessed July 12, 2022).

3. Again, I'm hedging. I can't remember a war game that ended poorly, with no insights generated.

4. John Horn, "Playing War Games to Win," *McKinsey Quarterly* (March 2011).

5. See, for example, Kevin Werbach and Dan Hunter, *For the Win: The Power of Gamification and Game Thinking in Business, Education, Government, and Social Impact* (Philadelphia: Wharton School Press, 2012).

6. Micah Zenko, *Red Team: How to Succeed by Thinking Like the Enemy* (New York: Basic Books, 2015).

Chapter 7

1. National Commission on Terrorist Attacks upon the United States, *The 9/11 Commission Report: Final Report of the National Commission on Terrorist Attacks upon the United States* (Washington, DC: National Commission on Terrorist Attacks upon the United States, 2004).

2. *The 9/11 Commission Report, Executive Summary*, 10–11.

3. *The 9/11 Commission Report, Executive Summary*, 13.

4. *The 9/11 Commission Report, Executive Summary*, 24.

5. This naming convention was suggested by the financial services executive at the company discussed in this chapter.

6. See also Tetlock and Gardner, *Superforecasting*, 193–210.

7. I used the search terms "strategy," "corporate development," "business development," "growth," "innovation," "M&A," "planning," and "transformation" to identify whether a listed executive had a strategic responsibility. Some of the executive bios indicated they had previous strategy responsibility at the vice president or senior vice president level but not in their current leadership role, and they were not included in the count (nor were their companies if none of the other executives had a strategic role). I excluded all CEOs and presidents from the list (unless they also had another C-Suite leadership title that indicated strategy responsibility). Financial institutions more commonly had a chief risk officer than a CSO (I did not include the CRO as a "strategy" role). Finally, not all company websites included executive bios or current responsibilities; this was much more common with foreign-owned firms.

8. Richard H. Thaler and Cass R. Sunstein, *Nudge: Improving Decisions about Health, Wealth, and Happiness* (New Haven, CT: Yale University Press, 2009).

9. Thanks to Kevin Farr and Michael Hsiung for brainstorming with me on how to build a competitive insight dashboard.

Index

Page numbers followed by f refer to figures.